The Authority Effect

Four weeks to Speak Life, Heal the Sick, and Live Powerfully in the Spirit

by

Holly Bogdan

This book is a work of nonfiction based on the author's personal experiences and biblical interpretation. It is intended to inspire, encourage, and equip readers in their spiritual journey. While every effort has been made to ensure scriptural accuracy, the content should not be substituted for pastoral counsel or theological training.

ISBN: 979-8-9997091-1-0
Printed in the United States of America
First Edition

Dedication

To my dad—
the one who encourages me when I'm down,
prays for me when I'm lost,
and loves me no matter what.
Thank you for walking this journey with me.

Table of Contents

Welcome to My Simple, yet Supernatural Life

Welcome, I'm so glad you're here.

Whether you've walked with Jesus for many years or are just beginning to ask how God is moving today, this devotional is meant for you. It's no accident you're holding it…God has a purpose in placing it in your hands. I believe God sent this devotional your way for a reason.

You were never meant to just survive this life. You were created to **release heaven on earth**.

Over the past decade, I've stumbled, stretched, and grown into a life I once thought was reserved for pastors, prophets, or "the bold ones." But I've come to learn something that changed everything:

The supernatural life isn't for a select few.

It's for ***every believer****. That means…it's for* ***you too****.*

John Bevere recently said, "If you don't walk in your God-given authority, the enemy will seek to take it away and use it against you."

That's where this daily devotional comes in—to help you understand your authority in Christ. This 4-week journey is filled with personal stories, scriptural teaching, and simple practical exercises designed to help you **hear God's voice, release His healing, and live with boldness.**

Each week, there are six daily devotionals (even God needed a day off!) which build on the week before:

- Week 1: My Identity in Christ
- Week 2: Hearing God's Voice
- Week 3: You Can Heal the Sick
- Week 4: Listen & Obey

So, take a deep breath, open your heart, and get ready—because once you realize what you carry, everything changes.

You don't have to be loud. You don't have to have a platform. You just have to be willing.

"If you are willing and obedient, You shall eat the good of the land."

— **Isaiah 1:19 (NKJV)**

My Testimony

I first encountered Jesus when I was six years old. I couldn't explain theology or answer every question about the mechanics of salvation, but I *knew* He loved me—and somehow, I knew I could trust Him with my whole life.

Over the years, that simple knowing became something more: a lifestyle of hearing His voice, obedience, doing his word, laying hands on the sick, and watching healing miracles unfold in the most ordinary places—at the dentist's chair, restaurants, breakrooms, even the produce aisle at the grocery store. I call it "my simple, yet supernatural life," because to me, living this way should be normal for every believer.

Why I Wrote This Devotional

I never set out to become a "healer" or a "healing teacher." I was just a corporate professional with a growing hunger to see more of God in my everyday life. When I started blogging about my experiences, I was amazed by how many people responded—not just with encouragement, but with questions. *Can I do this too? How? Where do I even begin?*

That's why I wrote this devotional: to share what I've learned and to walk with you as you discover it for yourself. Each day offers stories, scripture, and practical steps to help you hear God's voice, pray with boldness, and watch His kingdom transform even the smallest corners of your life.

The Power of Testimony

You'll notice that this devotional is built around real stories: testimonies of healing, bold faith, unexpected provision, and supernatural encounters. That's not accidental. It's intentional. Testimonies carry power—they speak life into weary hearts and prove that God's Word still works. When we share what He's done, we make room for Him to do it again.

The word **testimony** comes from a Hebrew root word 'edut' that means **"do it again."** When we share what God has done, we're not just remembering—we're inviting it to happen again, in our lives and in the lives of others. Testimonies are prophetic in nature. They release faith into the atmosphere and declare that if God did it once, He can do it again.

Psalm 77:11 (NKJV) reads:

"I will remember the works of the Lord; Surely I will remember Your wonders of old."

When you hear someone else's miracle, you don't have to just admire it—you can claim it. The same Spirit who healed, restored, and provided for them is alive in you.

"For the testimony of Jesus is the spirit of prophecy." —Revelation 19:10 (NKJV)

That means every story of what Jesus has done carries power to release what He's still doing. So, as you read each entry, don't just skim. Pause. Receive. Agree. Say, "Me too, Lord."

And remember, one day someone might point to your story as the moment their faith came alive. Your testimony could be the breakthrough they've been waiting for. Your testimony might be the next one someone else claims as their breakthrough. And remember, your story isn't just your own—it's a seed. One day, someone will read your testimony and recognize their own miracle waiting to happen. What God begins in you, He will continue through you.

Before You Begin: A Personal Invitation

The supernatural life is available to all believers—but it starts with a relationship. If you're not sure where you stand with God, or whether you've truly invited Jesus into your life, this is the most important place to start.

Scripture tells us that salvation isn't complicated or reserved for the perfect. It says:

"If you declare with your mouth, 'Jesus is Lord,' and believe in your heart that God raised Him from the dead, you will be saved."
—Romans 10:9 (NIV)

Don't turn another page without settling that first. "If you feel that tug in your heart, that's Jesus inviting you closer. Don't ignore it—respond now."

The supernatural power this devotional speaks of—the miracles, the healings, and the authority—is all possible because of the Holy Spirit living within us. Jesus promised that when He returned to the Father, He would send us the ultimate Helper:

"Very truly I tell you, whoever believes in Me will do the works I have been doing, and they will do even greater things than these, because I am going to the Father."

—John 14:12 (NIV)

He followed that promise with this:

"And I will ask the Father, and He will give you another Helper, to be with you forever—the Spirit of truth... He lives with you and will be in you."

—John 14:16–17 (NIV)

The same Spirit who raised Jesus from the dead now lives in you—and He's the One who will lead, guide, and empower you through every page of this devotional.

The Believer's Prayer

You can pray this out loud right now—He's listening:

Jesus, I believe You are the Son of God. I believe You died on the cross for my sins and rose again to give me eternal life. I confess that I need You. I turn from my old ways and ask You to be the Lord of my life. I receive Your forgiveness and grace. I also ask You to fill me with Your Holy Spirit—baptize me in power so I can live the life You've called me to. I want everything You have for me. Thank You for saving me. In Jesus' name, Amen.

Week 1: My Identity in Christ

"Your purpose flows from your identity, not your activity. You're not trying to discover what you should do for God—you're learning who you are in Christ and letting purpose emerge from that reality."

—**Graham Cooke**

Everything in the Christian life begins here—knowing who you are in Christ. Before you can hear His voice, heal the sick, or walk boldly in the Spirit, you must be rooted in identity—not performance. You are not powerless, overlooked, or unqualified; you are a child of God, filled with His Spirit and entrusted with His authority.

Over this coming week, you'll:

- Discover what's already yours in Christ and learn to walk in it with confidence.
- Recognize that hearing God's voice is your spiritual birthright.
- See that even the smallest attacks must bow to Jesus' name.
- Understand that your words carry supernatural power to move mountains.
- Embrace freedom through forgiveness and recognize the gifts already in your hands.
- Shift your prayers from pleading to declaring the finished work of the cross.

By the end of these six days, you'll realize that living supernaturally isn't about striving for something new, it's about awakening to what you already carry.

2 Peter 1:3 (NKJV)

"As His divine power has given to us all things that pertain to life and godliness, through the knowledge of Him who called us by glory and virtue."

Day 1: Supernatural Starts Here

Scripture Anchor

John 10:27 (NKJV) –

"My sheep hear My voice, and I know them, and they follow Me."

My Story

God loves us so much!

"See what great love the Father has lavished on us, that we should be called children of God!" – 1 John 3:1 (NIV)

I was six years old when I knew God loved me. Not because of a sermon or a Sunday school handout—but because I felt it. In the way a child knows the sky is blue or the sun is warm, I just *knew*. I couldn't explain it, but I wanted more. I wanted to belong to Jesus.

As I grew older, that sense of closeness never really left. Sure, I had teenage rebellion and adult distractions. I made mistakes, doubted, and went through seasons where God felt far. But underneath it all, I always had this whisper in my spirit: *He's still here.*

Somewhere along the way, I realized that "hearing God's voice" wasn't reserved for prophets or preachers...I didn't need to be on a stage or go to seminary to hear God's voice. I just needed to know I had the gift of the Holy Spirit and be willing to listen. That voice wasn't thunderous or dramatic. It was a nudge. A knowing. A thought I hadn't thought. A gentle reminder that I belonged to someone bigger than my circumstances.

Often, God speaks through His Word, through a sudden sense of peace or conviction, through an inner impression, or through the quiet confirmation of Scripture. Learning to hear Him isn't about chasing signs—it's about becoming familiar with His presence and trusting that He still speaks today.

As I began studying healing, I understood that I had everything I already needed to pray for others. That I could stand on the promises from the Bible, that anything Jesus did while on earth, I could do too. The first time I felt prompted to pray for someone in a restaurant, my heart raced! What if I was wrong about what I was hearing? What if I embarrassed myself? But I couldn't shake the feeling, so I obeyed. I offered a simple prayer. And God showed up.

From that point forward—the moment I confessed Jesus Christ as Lord —the supernatural stopped being something I admired from a distance and started becoming part of my daily rhythm. Healing. Direction. Boldness. Peace. Not because I was special, but because I was *available.*

"Then I heard the voice of the Lord saying, 'Whom shall I send? And who will go for us?' And I said, 'Here am I. Send me!'" **Isaiah 6:8 (NIV)**

Reflection

The supernatural life isn't flashy. It's not about theatrics or perfection. It's about partnership.

Jesus said His sheep would hear His voice. That means hearing Him is part of your spiritual DNA—not something you have to earn or strive for. If you belong to Jesus, then hearing His voice is already your birthright.

"My sheep listen to my voice; I know them, and they follow me." **John 10:27 (NIV)**

The Bible shows us that God *has always been a communicator*. He spoke to Adam in the garden, called out to Moses from a burning bush, and whispered to Elijah in a still, small voice. Through Jesus, God made His desire for relationship even more personal: "The Word became flesh and dwelt among us" (John 1:14). After Jesus ascended, He gave us the Holy Spirit to dwell within us and continue that communication.

1 Corinthians 2:12 (NKJV) says, *"Now we have received...the Spirit who is from God, that we might know the things that have been freely given to us by God."*

Did you catch that? The Holy Spirit was given so we might *know*—not guess or wonder but *know* what God has given us.

But like any relationship, closeness grows through connection. When we invite God into the everyday—our car rides, our grocery runs, our meetings and mealtimes—His voice becomes easier to recognize. It might feel subtle at first, but with practice, it becomes unmistakable.

Reflective Question

Where in my life today is God inviting me to pause and listen for His voice?

Activation Prayer

Jesus, I believe You still speak today—and that I can hear You. Thank You for giving me ears to hear and a heart to respond. I repent for any agreement I've made with the lie that You're silent, distant, or only speak to "more spiritual people."

Holy Spirit, teach me to quiet the noise and tune in to Your voice. I receive the truth that I am Your sheep, and You are my Shepherd. I don't have to chase signs or feelings—I simply have to follow You. Speak, Lord. I'm listening.

Daily Challenge (Muscle Builder #1)

Step 1: Set a 5-minute timer today and find a quiet space. Ask God one question:

"What do You want me to know today?"

Step 2: Write down whatever comes—whether it's a word, a picture, a scripture, or a feeling. Don't judge it. Don't filter it. Just write it down below.

Step 3: Then ask a follow-up: **"Is there someone You want me to encourage today?"**

If someone comes to mind, send a message or say a prayer for them. This is how the supernatural becomes part of your natural life. Jot their name down here, and during this journey, see if your prayer makes a difference in their life.

Day 2: Bugs Can't Hurt Me

Scripture Anchor

Mark 16:17–18 (NKJV) –

"And these signs will follow those who believe: In My name they will cast out demons…they will lay hands on the sick, and they will recover…and if they drink anything deadly, it will by no means hurt them."

My Story

As a child, I was the kind of kid who swelled up dramatically from every mosquito bite. My skin would react in big, itchy, red welts—and I just accepted it as normal. But something changed once I learned what Jesus meant when He said, *"Nothing shall by any means hurt you."*

It started small. One day I was out in the yard and got bitten. I remembered the scripture in Mark 16 and thought: *"Why am I accepting this? Jesus gave me authority over sickness and attacks." "Jesus gave me authority to stand against sickness and every form of attack."* So, I did something I had never done before—I spoke to the bite.

"In Jesus' name, this bite must leave. I declare my body is protected by the blood of Jesus. No swelling. No itching. No reaction. You don't get to stay."

And that was it. The reaction never came.

From then on, I started practicing this, every time I felt a symptom try to land on me—whether it was a cold, headache, sore throat, or anxiety. I stopped talking about symptoms and started talking *to* them. That's right…I began to speak *to* the problem. Jesus' instruction on this point is in Mark 11:23 (NIV): *"Truly I tell you, if anyone says to this mountain, 'Go, throw yourself into the sea,' and does not doubt in their heart but believes that what they say will happen, it will be done for them."*

Does that mean I never feel unwell? No. But the moment a symptom shows up, I no longer assume it's mine. I don't claim it. I resist it. I take authority over the sickness or attack and tell it go. And more often than not, it leaves before it can take hold.

Reflection

This may sound radical, but it's actually just biblical. Jesus never told us to tolerate the enemy's attacks - He modeled how to confront them in faith.

Luke 10:19 (NKJV) says:
"Behold, I give you the authority…over all the power of the enemy, and nothing shall by any means hurt you."

When you realize that sickness, disease, fear, and pain are attacks—not divine lessons—you begin to respond with authority instead of resignation. Jesus didn't just die for your salvation—He died for your wholeness. *"By His stripes we are healed"* (Isaiah 53:5).

So why do symptoms still show up? Because we live in a fallen world with a real enemy. But that enemy is *defeated.* He only has access when we agree with his lies.

James 4:7 (NKJV) gives us a key:
"Submit to God. Resist the devil and he will flee from you."

The word **resist** in the original Greek is *anthistémi*, meaning "to actively oppose, to stand against." You don't resist something by tolerating it. You resist it by speaking truth—out loud and in faith.

That's what Jesus did. He spoke to storms. He spoke to trees. He spoke to fevers. And He told *us* to do the same: speak to the mountain and it will move.

Reflective Question

Where in my life today do I need to stop tolerating the enemy's attack and start speaking God's truth in faith?

Activation Prayer

Jesus, thank You for giving me authority in Your name. I repent for every time I've partnered with fear, tolerated sickness, or accepted defeat as "normal." I receive the truth today that You have given me dominion over every scheme of the enemy.

Holy Spirit, train me to recognize the first signs of an attack—and to respond swiftly with the Word of God. I declare that my body is not a playground for affliction. I am healed by the blood of

Jesus, sealed by the Spirit, and filled with resurrection power. I resist every lie, and I stand in divine health. In Jesus' name, amen.

Daily Challenge (Muscle Builder #2)

Step 1: Pay attention to your body today. If any symptom—however small—tries to show up (a headache, allergy, fatigue, soreness), **speak out loud**:

"In Jesus' name, I rebuke this [symptom]. You have no place in my body. I resist you, and you must go."

Step 2: When you encounter a friend or coworker who casually says, "I'm coming down with something" or "My allergies are acting up," don't ignore it. **Quietly pray for them in your spirit**, or if the moment is right, offer a gentle response like:

"Can I pray for you? I really believe healing is part of what Jesus paid for."

Step 3: Use the space below to journal the result. Did the symptoms leave? Did someone respond to your offer? Track what God is doing as you start to walk in His authority.

Day 3: Speak to the Mountain

Scripture Anchor

Mark 11:23 (NKJV) –

"For assuredly, I say to you, whoever ***says*** *to this mountain, 'Be removed and be cast into the sea,' and does not doubt in his heart… he will have whatever he* ***says****."*

My Story

When I first met my husband, he had persistent knee pain. His default solution was Advil—and avoiding some of his favorite things like running and cycling.

I began to teach him about his authority in Christ and how to speak to pain directly, commanding it to leave.

The first time I taught someone to speak healing over their own body, they almost always feel a little silly. But the truth is, the body responds to both faith and words.

Often after I pray for someone, they feel great, for a while. But then the pain returns. Why? Because pain is an attack from the enemy, and like a thief who once broke into your house, he'll try to come back, especially if he thinks he still has access.

One morning, after enjoying a couple pain-free days, my husband woke up and felt that old familiar ache in his knee. But this time, instead of reaching for medication or giving in to frustration, he sat up, placed his hand on his knee, and spoke with confidence:

"Pain, you are not welcome here and I command you to leave. Knee, be restored. I am healed by the stripes of Jesus."

It wasn't fancy or emotional—but it was *faithful*. As he spoke, the pain began to lift. Minutes later, it was gone.

That moment sparked a new habit: speaking healing over himself as a first response—not a last resort.

Now, when something flares up—a sore throat, inflammation, or tight muscles—he doesn't panic or power through. He pauses, speaks the Word, and reminds the enemy: *You don't live here anymore.*

If you've lived with pain for a long time, your body may have grown used to it. It's like a squatter: the longer it stays, the more it feels at home. Even after you kick it out, if no one confronts it again, it might settle right back in.

That's why it's okay to pray more than once. You're not begging God—you're standing your ground. You're reminding the thief: *You're not welcome here anymore.*

Reflection

God's healing power is not confined to church services or altar calls.
It moves when **faith and the Word collide**—anywhere, anytime.

Psalm 107:20 says: "He sent His Word and healed them…"

It doesn't say He sent a preacher. Or a prophet. It says He sent **His Word.** That means His Word is the carrier of healing—and **you can release it.**

Your voice is a weapon.

Jesus didn't beg God to heal people—He **spoke** to bodies, to storms, to spirits. He showed us what authority looks like:

- "Be healed."
- "Rise and walk."
- "Peace, be still."
- "Stretch out your hand."

You're called to do the same.

If you wait to feel powerful before you speak, you'll stay silent. But if you speak the Word *even when it feels awkward or weak,* power gets released.

When you speak healing over your own body, you're not being presumptuous—you're being *biblical.* You're aligning your words with God's Word. That's the kind of faith that moves mountains.

The truth is that your body has been listening to your words for years. Science and Scripture both affirm this.

Biblically, Proverbs 18:21 tells us:

"Death and life are in the power of the tongue, and those who love it will eat its fruit." (NKJV)

Scientifically, research in neuroscience and psycho-neuroimmunology shows that your words have a measurable effect on your brain and body.

The limbic system—the emotional center of your brain—responds to what you repeatedly say and think, activating physical responses such as stress, inflammation, or healing processes. Your body literally builds pathways based on your spoken patterns over time.

So let me ask you: What have you been saying to your body?

Have you been saying…

- "I always get sick this time of year."
- "This runs in my family, so it makes sense it's happening to me."
- "I'll probably deal with this forever."

Those aren't just complaints, they're **agreements.** And what we agree with, we empower. What if your own words have been supporting and promoting the very things God wants to heal?

It's time to speak something new.

You don't need eloquence. You need **authority.** You already have it. Now it's time to use it. Luke 10:19 agrees: "Behold, I give you the authority to trample on serpents and scorpions, and over all the power of the enemy, and nothing shall by any means hurt you." (NKJV)

Reflective Question

What "mountain" in my life today do I need to speak God's truth to and watch it move?

Activation Prayer

Father, thank You that Your Word carries healing power. I don't need the perfect setting or mood—I just need faith and my voice.

Jesus, You paid for my healing. You showed me how to live in authority. I choose to follow Your example.

Holy Spirit, help me speak truth even when I feel weak. Train my mouth to agree with Heaven. Let my words carry breakthrough—for myself and for others.

I declare I am healed, whole, and aligned with the finished work of Jesus. In His name I pray, amen.

Daily Challenge (Muscle Builder #3)

Step 1: Identify one symptom in your body today.
Whether minor (headache, tension, fatigue) or chronic, write it down in the space below.

Step 2: Look up a healing scripture that counters it.
Suggestions: Isaiah 53:5, Psalm 103:2–3, 1 Peter 2:24

Step 3: Speak out loud to that symptom.
Try this template:

"In Jesus' name, I speak to this [symptom]. You are trespassing. I declare that by His stripes, I am healed. I command this [symptom] to leave now. Body, line up with Heaven."

Repeat it throughout the day. Don't beg—**believe.**

Track it: What shifted in your body? What shifted in your *faith*? Write down any testimonies you can share with others.

Day 4: The Power to Forgive

Scripture Anchor

Matthew 18:35 (NKJV) –
"So My heavenly Father also will do to you if each of you, from his heart, does not forgive his brother his trespasses."

My Story

Forgiveness is rarely straightforward.

Unfortunately, my first marriage ended in divorce. I had amazing support from friends and family who kept me 'supernaturally buoyant' after the dust had settled. I thought I had processed most of the pain. I understood why my ex-husband left, and I'd done the hard work of letting that go. But there was another wound that lingered—one I hadn't fully acknowledged.

His sister. My former sister-in-law.

For nearly two decades, she had been like family. At every holiday, every milestone, every memory—she was there. I had even written her into my will as the guardian for my daughter, trusting her to be our safe place if anything ever happened to me.

And then, quietly, she disappeared from our lives.

There was no big conflict. No dramatic falling out. Just silence. And in that silence, it felt like my daughter and I had been abandoned.

Every time I heard a sermon on forgiveness, I thought: *Not yet. She should apologize. She should reach out. Then I'll forgive.* But that day never came.

One night, I revisited a chapter in M. James Jordan's *Sonship: A Journey into the Father's Heart*. In it, he offered a "formula" for forgiving from the heart—not just with the will, but with compassion. It began with something simple and profound:

You can't release a debt you haven't named.

So I sat down and listed everything I'd lost: her presence in our lives, the safety net I counted on for my daughter, the emotional weight I'd carried alone. And then I asked a deeper question: *Could she even repay it?*

The answer was no.

She couldn't give me back the years, the holidays, the sense of stability I thought we'd have.

But when I imagined the brokenness she might be carrying, compassion cracked open the door.

And through that door, the Holy Spirit walked in.

In that moment, I forgave her—not because she earned it, but because I was finally ready to release the pain God had been waiting to heal.

Reflection

Forgiveness isn't about pretending it didn't hurt or erasing the memory. It's about releasing the weight of the debt and letting God be the healer of what was broken.

Jesus taught this through a story in Matthew 18. A servant is forgiven a massive debt by his master—yet refuses to forgive someone else for a much smaller one. When the master finds out, he says, *"Should you not also have had compassion...?"*

Then Jesus says something sobering:
"So My heavenly Father also will do to you if each of you, from his heart, does not forgive."

This kind of forgiveness isn't surface-level. It's not just saying the words. It's a release that begins with naming what was taken, recognizing it can't be repaid, and choosing to see the other person with **God's eyes**—not yours.

To further reinforce this, we need to realize that forgiveness begins when we dare to name what was taken, acknowledge it can't be repaid, and chose to see through God's eyes, not our own.

It's not easy. But it's freedom.

Forgiveness doesn't mean trust is instantly restored. It doesn't mean justice is ignored. It means *you get to stop bleeding internally* while waiting for someone else to acknowledge the wound.

You're not letting them off the hook. You're letting **yourself** off the hook.

You don't have to wait for someone to apologize before you heal. **Jesus didn't.**

Reflective Question

Who is it in my life today do I need to complete forgive and let go of the debt?

Activation Prayer

Jesus, You forgave me when I didn't even ask. You absorbed the debt I could never repay. Now I ask for the courage to extend that same mercy to others.

Holy Spirit, reveal any area in my heart where I'm still holding forgiveness. Help me name what was taken. Show me what I've carried that You never asked me to.

Give me eyes to see the one who hurt me as You see them—broken, beloved, redeemable. I forgive them today—not to excuse the pain, but to release it. Not to let them go, but to let *myself* go.

Thank You that I don't have to carry this anymore. I release the debt. I choose freedom. In Jesus' name, amen.

Daily Challenge (Muscle Builder #4)

Step 1: Make a short list.
Ask the Holy Spirit: *"Who do I still need to forgive?"*
Write their names in the space below. Don't overthink—just be honest.

Step 2: Name the debt.
For each person, write what they took from you. (Trust? Time? Relationship? Security?)

Step 3: Release them out loud.

"Jesus, I forgive [name]. They cannot repay me, but I release them. I bless them. I choose peace."

Optional Support: Revisit Matthew 18:21–35 and let Jesus walk you through it.

Step 4: Journal any emotions or physical shifts below. Forgiveness can unlock hidden tension, pain, or grief. Let it come. Let it go.

Day 5: What's in Your Hand?

Scripture Anchor

Exodus 4:2 (NIV) –
"Then the Lord said to him, 'What is that in your hand?' 'A staff,' he replied."

My Story

I used to shrink back whenever someone mentioned "spiritual gifts".

I wasn't the one holding a microphone. I didn't lead worship. I didn't have a theology degree. I didn't see myself as a preacher. I loved God, but in the back of my mind, I always wondered: *What do I really have to offer?*

The people I admired seemed to shine on big platforms. They looked confident, called, and—frankly—far more spiritual than I felt. I started believing the lie that I was just "support staff" in the Kingdom. Faithful, maybe—but not *powerful*.

And then one day, while reading Exodus 4, a single line stood up and shouted at me.

God had just called Moses to lead the Israelites out of Egypt.
Moses panicked:
"What if they don't believe me?"
"I'm not eloquent."
"Send someone else."

And God replies with a question:

"What is that in your hand?"

A staff.
Just a stick. Something Moses had probably carried for years without thinking twice.

But that *ordinary* staff became the very tool God used to part seas, shatter enemy plans, and perform signs and wonders in front of nations.

That question didn't just challenge Moses, it started echoing in me:

What's in your hand?

I looked around at my life. I didn't have a pulpit, but I had a voice.
I didn't have credentials, but I had compassion.
I didn't have a big stage, but I had a prayer life.
I had time.
I had words.
I had hospitality.
I had love.

When I offered those simple things to God, He breathed on them—and I began to see lives shift, atmospheres change, and hearts healed.

Reflection

We often underestimate the everyday tools God has already placed in our lives. But He's not looking for perfection —He's looking for willingness. Moses didn't need to level up before saying yes. He just had to *offer what he already had.*

What if the "ordinary" in your life is exactly what God wants to use for something extraordinary?

In Exodus 4, Moses only had a shepherd's staff. But that was the very thing God used to:

- Part a sea
- Strike a rock
- Demonstrate power
- Defeat Pharaoh's magicians

God didn't need a polished résumé—He needed a *willing heart.*

You might think you don't have "ministry tools" in your hand. But what if…

- That notebook is your first devotional?
- That dinner table is your first discipleship group?
- That text message is your first prophetic word?
- That compassion is your open door to healing ministry?

What's in your hand *today* may look small—but with God, **it multiplies.**

So instead of saying, "I'm not enough," start asking, "God, how do You want to use what I already have?"

Reflective Question

What simple gift, resource, or ability in my hand today could God be inviting me to surrender so He can multiply it?

Activation Prayer

Father, thank You that I don't need to be impressive—I just need to be available. You never asked for perfection, only surrender.

Jesus, show me what's already in my hand. Remind me that nothing I give to You is too small for Your Kingdom. Multiply my simple offerings. Stretch my faith.

Holy Spirit, open my eyes to see what's in my hand. Reveal the hidden value in what I've overlooked—my time, my voice, my relationships, my presence. I surrender them to You. Use them to bring healing, hope, and transformation. I give You what I have and ask You to do what only You can do with it. In Jesus' name, Amen.

Daily Challenge (Muscle Builder #5)

Step 1: List what's "in your hand" right now.
Make a list of the gifts, skills, resources, and opportunities that are already in your hand—things you've perhaps taken for granted:

- What do you enjoy?
- What do people come to you for?
- What has God already given you access to?

Step 2: Ask God to show you how to use one of those things for His glory—today.
Example: If you're a good listener, reach out to someone who needs to talk. If you're creative, make something encouraging for someone else.

Step 3: Write what you did—and how it felt in the space below.
Step out! Send the text, speak the encouragement, offer your help, or pray for someone. Watch what God does with your *yes*.

Declaration: "God, You've already placed everything I need in my hands. I don't have to wait to be used. I choose to offer You what I have today, trusting You to breathe on it and multiply it for Your glory."

Day 6: When Prayer Becomes a Declaration

Scripture Anchor

Isaiah 53:4-5 (NKJV) –

"Surely He has borne our griefs and carried our sorrows…but He was wounded for our transgressions, He was bruised for our iniquities; the chastisement for our peace was upon Him, and by His stripes ***we are healed****."*

My Story

I've met so many people who love Jesus, believe in healing, and genuinely pray in faith. Yet they're exhausted—their prayers sound like begging, their faith feels like striving, and when healing doesn't come instantly, they assume they've failed somehow.

I've been there too. I cried, fasted, pleaded, and tried to "build my faith" as if it were some kind of spiritual transaction—thinking that if I just said the right words or believed hard enough, maybe God would heal me.

But one day, while praying yet again for the same healing, I sensed the Holy Spirit interrupt me:

"Why are you asking Me to do what I've already done?"

That question changed everything.

I opened my Bible to Isaiah 53. I'd read it countless times a hundred times. But this time, I saw it with new eyes:

"By His stripes we *are* healed."
Not "*we might be.*"
Not "*might be if you pray long enough.*"
But **are.** Present tense. Already. Done.

Healing isn't something we try to convince God to do—it's something Jesus **already paid for**.

The New Testament is full of moments where believers didn't ask God to heal someone—they **commanded healing to manifest**:

- Peter said, *"In the name of Jesus Christ of Nazareth, rise up and walk"* (Acts 3:6).
- Jesus often rebuked the sickness or cast out the spirit with a word.
- The disciples "laid hands on the sick, and they recovered" (Mark 16:18).

They weren't trying to convince God. They were **agreeing with what He already promised**.

That's the difference between asking and declaring.

When you ask, you're acknowledging need.
When you declare, you're standing in authority—trusting that the provision is already complete in Jesus.

There's a time for both. But once you've asked and believed, it's not only okay— it's necessary—to shift into declaration. You're not commanding God, you're commanding the situation to **align with God's Word.**

Reflection

Are your prayers filled with striving, or with trust?
Have you been begging God to do something He already finished on the cross?

Many of us without realizing approach healing—and other promises of God—as if we have to convince Him.

We pray like this:

- "Please heal me…"
- "God, if it's Your will…"
- "Do something, Lord…"

But what if He already did? We pray prayers God already answered two-thousand years ago on the cross. Healing is not a reward for perfect performance—it's an **inheritance** for every believer who trusts in Jesus.

Isaiah 53 says healing was included in the same work that forgave your sins.
Just like you don't beg to be forgiven—you **receive** it—healing is received, not negotiated.

When Jesus said on the cross, *"It is finished,"* He wasn't just talking about sin. He meant **all of it**:

- Your peace
- Your healing
- Your redemption
- Your access to the Father

This isn't name-it-claim-it theology – it's resting on covenant truth We don't manipulate outcome; we agree with what Christ has already done.

You're not trying to earn healing. You're stepping into what Jesus *already paid for.* So today, stop pleading for what's already yours – stand up, speak His Word and declare what He has finished.

Reflective Question

Where have my prayers become striving and begging—and how can I shift them into bold declarations of God's finished work today?

Activation Prayer

Jesus, thank You for the finished work of the cross. Thank You that You didn't die only for my sin, but for my healing, my peace, my wholeness.

Forgive me for approaching You like You're withholding something I have to earn. I choose to stop striving—and start agreeing with what You've already done.

Holy Spirit, teach me to pray with boldness and clarity. Show me when to ask, when to thank, and when to declare. I trust in the finished work of the cross, and I align my words with Heaven's truth. Let every cell in my body, and every thought in my mind, come into agreement with Your will.

I receive it. I thank You for it. I declare that by Your stripes, I *am* healed.
Not someday. Not maybe. But already.

Let that truth renew my mind and shift my prayers—from pleading to proclaiming. In Jesus' name, amen.

Daily Challenge (Muscle Builder #6)

Step 1: Read Isaiah 53:4–5 and 1 Peter 2:24.
Read them out loud. Replace "we" with *your name.* Declare it with conviction.

Step 2: Identify where you've been striving.
Are you begging God for something He's already accomplished? Switch your language from asking to *thanking* and *declaring.*

Step 3: Write this down on a sticky note and say it daily:

"Healing isn't coming—it's **already done**. I am healed because Jesus already paid the price."

Declaration:

"Jesus, I thank You that by Your stripes I am healed. I don't have to beg or plead—I simply believe and receive. I declare that my body, my mind, and my spirit are aligned with Your Word. Healing is mine in Jesus' name."

Week 2: Hearing God's Voice

"Hearing God's voice is easier and more natural than you think. You were born to live in connection with God, and the Holy Spirit is the One who enables that connection and ability to hear His voice." — ***Bill Johnson***

God's voice isn't distant or mysterious—it's woven into the very fabric of who you are. You were created to hear Him, not through striving, but through the simple, supernatural connection already provided by the Holy Spirit.

This week, you'll learn to attune your spirit to that gentle whisper—even amid the everyday chaos. Over this coming week, you'll:

- Sense God's peace in the storm and His clarity in the confusion.
- Recognize His guidance through whispers, confirmations, and divine alignment.
- Learn to live hand-in-hand with Him in everyday moments.
- Stop chasing an elusive "word" and instead rest in His steady leading.
- Grow in courage to obey His voice —even when it makes no human sense.
- Move from silence to steady communion, letting go of the fear of missing His voice.

By the end of these six days—you'll realize that being led by God isn't for a select few. It's your birthright in Christ. You aren't striving for a voice—you're awakening to the tune that's been playing for your entire life.

Day 7: Daughter of the King

Scripture Anchor

Romans 8:16–17 (NKJV) –
"The Spirit Himself bears witness with our spirit that we are children of God, and if children, then heirs—heirs of God and joint heirs with Christ..."

My Story

We were getting ready to sell our house, and I knew I didn't want to make a move without God's direction. So I prayed, and the Holy Spirit gave me a specific number—clear, quiet, and higher than anything the market suggested.

When I shared it with our realtor, she hesitated. "That's really aggressive," she said. "I'd recommend listing lower."

But I couldn't shake what God had said.

I asked Him again—*Why this number?*
And in my spirit, I sensed His gentle reply:

Because I love you. Because I want to bless you. Because you're My daughter, and I care about the details of your life.

It wasn't about market strategy. It wasn't even just about money. It was about relationship.

This was a moment for me to respond to His love with obedience. Not to *earn* anything, but to *receive* what He wanted to give.

So I stood my ground—not arrogantly, but confidently. I said, "We'll list it at the number He gave me, and we'll wait until Sunday. That's when the right offer will come."

Sure enough, three offers came in—**on Sunday**—just as I'd heard.

It wasn't just about the money. It was about listening to the Holy Spirit and believing that what He says comes from love. As His daughter, I was entitled to every promise He had for me. And that obedience isn't a transaction—it's an act of agreement. It's saying, *Yes, Father. I believe You're good. I believe You see me. I'll act like I'm loved.*

That was the day I stopped calling it luck and started calling it *favor.*

"Favor isn't always about finances-it's about God's presence and alignment in every area of life."

Reflection

Many of us live like we're barely tolerated by God—like we're hired help in His household. But the truth is: **you are family.** You're not just saved—you're seated. Not just forgiven—but favored. You are a daughter of the King.

And daughters inherit.

Galatians 4:7 (NKJV) says:
"Therefore you are no longer a slave but a son, and if a son, then an heir of God through Christ."

Let that sink in. You are an **heir**—which means God wants you to live in the fullness of what Christ paid for: peace, healing, wisdom, provision, purpose, and power.

This isn't spiritual arrogance. It's spiritual alignment. You're not asking God for scraps—you're standing in His Word. You don't have to plead for things that are already yours in Christ. Instead, you *declare* what Heaven has already said is true.

But here's the challenge: if you don't know who you are, the enemy will tell you who you're not. He'll say you're unworthy, unqualified, too late, too much, too little. And if you believe him, you'll live like an orphan when you've already been adopted.

Today is about rejecting the lies and receiving your royal position.

Reflective Question

Where in my life today have I been living like an orphan instead of a daughter of the King, and how is God inviting me to step into my inheritance today?

Activation Prayer

Father, thank You that I am not a stranger to You—I am Your child. I receive the truth that I am not just saved from something, but saved *into* something. I am saved from sin into the family of God, into the royal family of God.

Holy Spirit, reveal to me any place where I have believed a lie about who I am. Break off every orphan mindset, every shame-based thought, every fear that says I'm not enough.

Jesus, I declare that I am a daughter of the King. I have access to the inheritance You bought for me with Your blood. I walk in confidence, not because of my resume, but because of my redemption. I lack nothing. I receive everything. In Jesus' name, amen.

Daily Challenge (Muscle Builder #7)

Step 1: Write this declaration on a sticky note:

"I am a daughter of the King. I have full access to Heaven's promises. I don't beg—I believe."

Place it somewhere you'll see it often.

Step 2: Pay attention to your self-talk today.
Any time you catch yourself saying something rooted in lack, shame, or fear, **stop and replace it with truth.**

Examples:

- From "I'm always messing this up" → to → "I'm learning and covered by grace."
- From "I could never do that" → to → "I'm empowered by the Spirit who raised Jesus from the dead."

Bonus: List 3 areas in the space below where you've felt disqualified in the past. Then write a scripture next to each one that tells you the truth.

Day 8: Peace in a Pandemic

Scripture Anchor

John 14:27 (NIV) –

"Peace I leave with you; my peace I give to you. I do not give to you as the world gives. Do not let your hearts be troubled and do not be afraid."

My Story

When the pandemic first hit, fear swept through the world like wildfire—headlines screamed, grocery shelves emptied and even the air felt heavy.

But in the middle of it, I heard God whisper:

"What are you going to carry—fear or peace?"

That question lingered.

I began making a deliberate choice: *I would be a peace-bringer, not a panic-spreader.*
So every time fear tried to sneak in through the news or social media, I would speak aloud:

"Jesus, You are my peace. I will not partner with fear. I choose to carry Your presence into this atmosphere."

Something shifted—not just inside me, but around me.

People started commenting: *"You seem calm. How are you not overwhelmed?"*
Those simple conversations opened doors for prayer, encouragement, and even healing.

It reminded me that when everything feels uncertain, the peace of God becomes *evidence*—proof that He is near. And when we carry that peace, people notice. They lean in. They ask questions. Not because we have all the answers, but because we're anchored in the One who does. Here are a few tangible ways I've learned to protect and release peace in anxious moments:

- **Start my day in stillness** – before checking the news or email, I open my hands and declare, *"Jesus, You are my peace."*
- **Fast from fear** – if a headline triggers anxiety, I turn it into intercession instead of stress.
- **Worship out loud** – even five minutes of singing along to worship songs shifts the atmosphere of my home.
- **Speak peace into a room** – silently or aloud, I'll say, *"Peace be here. Fear must go."*

Reflection

Jesus didn't say, *"I'll give you peace if the world is peaceful."* He said:

"The peace I give is not like the world's."

That means your peace doesn't come from perfect circumstances—it comes from **deep connection with God.**

And here's the secret: peace isn't passive.
It's a *weapon.*

Isaiah 26:3 says:

"You will keep in perfect peace those whose minds are stayed on You..."

That means you fight fear by fixing your focus.

Whether the crisis is global or personal—God has already given you what you need.
You carry a Kingdom that cannot be shaken (Hebrews 12:28).
And when the world is spinning, you become a *still place* in the storm.

Reflective Question

Where in my life today is God inviting me to carry and intercession instead of fear and anxiety?

Activation Prayer

Jesus, thank You that peace is not something I earn—it's a gift You freely give. You are my anchor when the world feels chaotic. I receive Your peace again today.

Forgive me for every time I've partnered with fear, worry, or control. I break agreement with anxiety, and I come under the covering of Your presence.

Holy Spirit, let Your peace rise within me—deeper than the noise, stronger than the storm. Let me carry that peace into every

room, every conversation, every crisis.
I will not be shaken. In Jesus' name, amen.

Daily Challenge (Muscle Builder #8)

Step 1: Notice what you're "feeding" on today.
Are you constantly consuming news, debates, or fearful conversations? Pause. Reset.

Step 2: Read John 14:27 and Isaiah 26:3 aloud.
Let them speak louder than the noise.

Step 3: Become a peace-bearer today.
Choose one situation where you will intentionally carry peace and write about the outcome in the space below.

- Calm a tense conversation
- Send a peaceful text to someone afraid
- Pray over a space (your home, office, car)

Declaration:

"I carry a peace the world cannot give—and cannot take away."

Day 9: Heaven on Earth

Scripture Anchor

Matthew 6:10 (NIV) –

"Your kingdom come, Your will be done, on earth as it is in heaven."

My Story

I'll never forget the day I prayed for a friend who was overwhelmed with anxiety. She had been crying for hours—unraveling under anxiety. Unsure how to help, I whispered, Holy Spirit, *how do I pray for her?*

And instantly, I heard a phrase in my spirit:

"Let it be on earth as it is in Heaven" from the Lord's Prayer.

It was gentle, but clear.

In Heaven, there's no sickness.
No depression.
No anxiety.
No betrayal.
No lack.
No broken identity.

And if Jesus told us to pray for that kind of Kingdom to come **here**, then He must've meant it's available now. I looked at my friend and said, "In Heaven, there's no fear. No torment. No mental chaos. And Jesus told us to pray for that reality to come here—now. So that's what we're going to do."

Then I prayed—not in desperation, but in alignment:

"Peace, come. Fear, go. In the name of Jesus, I command this mind to come into agreement with Heaven. No fear lives there, so no fear belongs here."

As I spoke those words, her breathing steadied. The tears stopped. Her whole posture relaxed—like she was finally able to rest.

It wasn't dramatic. It wasn't loud. But it was holy.

That day reminded me: when we listen to the Holy Spirit and pray as He leads, we're not just offering comfort—we're releasing the reality of Heaven into the lives of people God loves.

From that moment forward, I began declaring over every area of brokenness:

"Let it be on earth—as it is in Heaven."

And I started to watch alignment happen. Not always instantly, not always loudly. but deeply, faithfully, sometimes gradually—always supernaturally.

Reflection

The Hebrew concept of **shalom** means more than peace. It means **nothing missing, nothing broken.** It's the wholeness of God—the way things *should be*—the way they exist in Heaven now.

When Jesus taught us to pray, *"Your Kingdom come, Your will be done, on earth as it is in Heaven,"* He wasn't teasing us with Heaven. He was **inviting us into partnership.** The Kingdom of God is not just a destination—it's a **manifestation**. Wherever you invite His reign, healing comes. Peace settles. Chaos bows.

And this isn't just wishful thinking. Jesus said:

"Whatever you bind on earth will be bound in heaven, and whatever you loose on earth will be loosed in heaven." (Matthew 18:18 NKJV)

He was teaching us to agree with Heaven—to forbid what doesn't belong and to release what does.

We are not waiting for Heaven—we're releasing it. We don't just wait for Heaven - we invite its reality to break in.
And yes, the world is still broken. But the people of God are not powerless. We carry the answer inside us.

Romans 14:17 says the Kingdom is *righteousness, peace, and joy in the Holy Spirit.*
When you pray for Heaven on Earth, you're asking for more than comfort—you're calling for transformation.

Reflective Question

Where in my life today do I need to declare, "Let it be done on earth as it is in Heaven"?

Activation Prayer

Father, thank You that Your Kingdom is not far away—it's here, through Jesus. Thank You that I don't have to wait for Heaven to experience healing, peace, or wholeness.

Jesus, I declare Your words: Let Your Kingdom come. Let Your will be done—in my body, in my mind, in my relationships, in my city—as it is in Heaven.

Holy Spirit, reveal any place I've settled for brokenness. Teach me to live in full alignment with what You already paid for: nothing missing, nothing broken. Let me carry Heaven everywhere I go. In Jesus' name, amen.

Daily Challenge (Muscle Builder #9)

Step 1: Choose one area of your life that feels out of alignment. Is it physical health? Emotional peace? Family dynamics? Finances? Identify it and write it in the space below.

Step 2: Find a scripture that reflects God's heart for that area. Then declare out loud:

"Let it be in my life as it is in Heaven. In Jesus' name."

Step 3: Spend 5 minutes worshiping—not pleading. Thank God in advance for the wholeness He's bringing.

Declaration:

"I live in alignment with Heaven. I don't just wait for wholeness—I release it."

Day 10: Served

Scripture Anchor

John 13:14-15 (NIV) –
"Now that I, your Lord and Teacher, have washed your feet, you also should wash one another's feet. I have set you an example that you should do as I have done for you."

My Story

As Sandra prayed for me, the pain vanished. And it hasn't returned since. I am healed.

I'm usually the one pouring out—praying for others, encouraging strangers, stepping into bold faith moments. But this time, it was my turn to be served.

After moving to a new city, my family was "church shopping," trying to find the right community. One day, I saw a post about a golf tournament sponsored by a small, Spirit-filled church. That phrase caught my attention. I've always valued Spirit-filled churches because they equip you in the gifts of the Holy Spirit—healing, prophecy, prayer, discernment—and I knew that's what our family needed in this next season.

So we visited. That morning, we walked into a small, unassuming church and were greeted by a lovely couple, Sandra and her husband. They were warm, kind and inviting.

We enjoyed the service. But it was what happened *after* the service that marked me forever.

As we were walking out, Sandra approached and said, "This was our first week volunteering as greeters. During my prayer time this morning, I asked God to use me. His response was crystal clear—'*Pray for the woman in the blue dress. She doesn't think she deserves My best for her.*' You're in a blue dress. Does that word sound like it's for you?"

She hadn't even finished her sentence, and I was already crying.

For months I had been dealing with constant pain in my leg, the lingering result of a break from seven years earlier. Just a week prior, I had told my husband how sad I felt that I didn't have anyone in my life to pray healing for me the way I pray healing for others.

And now, standing in front of me, was a woman sent by God with a word tailor-made for my heart. I shared what I was going through, and Sandra didn't hesitate. She laid hands on me and prayed with boldness and compassion for healing to flow. I know the promises of God's word— *"They will lay hands on the sick, and they will recover."* (Mark 16:18)

Reflection

We love the idea of serving God—of praying for others, ministering in healing, teaching, and being vessels of His power. But what happens when **He wants to serve you?**

The story above is a reminder that we were never meant to do this journey alone being part of a Spirit-filled church family matters. It's not just community—it's biblical instruction:

'Is anyone among you sick? Let them call the elders of the church to pray over them and anoint them with oil in the name of the Lord. And the prayer offered in faith will make the sick person well; the Lord will raise them up. If they have sinned, they will be forgiven. Therefore, confess your sins to each other and pray for each other so that you may be healed. The prayer of a righteous person is powerful and effective.' James 5:14-16 (NIV)

Even Jesus, on the night of the Last Supper, knelt down to serve *His disciples.* When Peter tried to resist, Jesus answered:

"Unless I wash you, you have no part with me." John 13:8 (NIV)

Sometimes the greatest act of surrender is letting God minister to you through others.

You are not just a vessel. You are a beloved child. And your Father delights in pouring out His goodness on you.

That day in church reminded me:
I can't always be the miracle worker.
Sometimes I'm the one in need of a miracle.
Sometimes I'm the woman in the blue dress.

Reflective Question

Where in my life today could God be inviting me to let others minister to me, instead of always being the one to serve?

Activation Prayer

Jesus, thank You that You came to serve—not just the crowds, but *me.*

Forgive me for the moments I tried to earn Your love instead of receiving it freely.
I open my heart today to Your voice, Your comfort, and Your provision.
Make me sensitive to those around me—and teach me to serve from overflow, not burnout.

I receive Your best. Not because I've earned it…but because You're just that good.
Amen.

Daily Challenge (Muscle Builder #10)

Step 1: Ask the Holy Spirit—"Where am I still refusing to receive?"
Is it in relationships? Finances? Prayer? Write what you hear in the space below.

Step 2: Let someone minister to you today.
Receive prayer. Accept the help. Say yes when someone offers kindness.

Step 3: End this day by thanking God for the ways He's *served you.*
Then ask: "Who can I bless from this place of rest?"

Declaration:

"I am not just a vessel—I am a beloved child.
I receive God's best. And from that overflow, I will serve others well."

Day 11: My Sheep Hear My Voice

Scripture Anchor

Isaiah 30:21 (NKJV) –

"Your ears shall hear a word behind you, saying, 'This is the way, walk in it,' whenever you turn to the right hand or whenever you turn to the left."

My Story

I was at a restaurant one evening, trying to explain to a friend, who happens to be a former minister, how real and practical divine healing is. I had been through training, witnessed everyday healing miracles, and I thought he'd be thrilled to hear the stories. But instead, I hit a wall of skepticism.

So, I silently asked God for help: *"If You want to prove Your point, now would be a great time."*

That's when I noticed a woman sitting about six feet away. As clear as day, I heard in my spirit: **"Carpal Tunnel."**

It wasn't audible. It didn't come with flashing lights. Just a phrase dropped gently into my mind—one I hadn't been thinking. But I knew it was Him.

I nervously walked over and asked, "I know this is unusual, but do you happen to have Carpal Tunnel?"

Her eyes widened. "Yes! How did you know that?"

"I believe God told me. Would it be okay if I prayed for you?"

She agreed, and I offered a short prayer for healing. Nothing dramatic—just obedience.

And my friend? His whole demeanor changed. He had just witnessed a prophetic word in action—followed by bold faith. That moment wasn't just for the woman at the table. It was for *him.* It was also for him, and for me. It reminded me that the Holy Spirit isn't just with us—He's actively speaking.

Reflection

Many believers assume hearing God speak is rare, mystical, or reserved for pastors and prophets. But Scripture paints a different picture:
"My sheep hear My voice" (John 10:27 NKJV).
That means if you belong to Jesus, *you can hear Him.*

He speaks through His Word. Through impressions. Through people. Through peace. Through warnings. Through dreams. Even through what seems like "random thoughts."

The Bible is filled with ordinary people who heard from God in practical ways. Ananias (Acts 9) received instructions to go lay hands on Saul. Philip (Acts 8) was told to walk alongside a stranger's chariot. Peter was told to go to the home of a Gentile, which changed church history.

The key wasn't perfection—it was *availability.* These men listened, then acted.

God's voice is often *still and small* (1 Kings 19:12 NKJV), which is why quieting the noise matters. That voice will always align with Scripture, and it will never lead you into fear or pride. The more you respond to it, the more confident you'll become.

Reflective Question

Where in my life today is God whispering a gentle nudge that I've been overlooking?

Activation Prayer

Father, I believe You speak to Your children—and that includes me. Forgive me for believing the lie that I'm not spiritual enough to hear from You. I silence the voices of doubt, fear, and self-judgment, and I choose to believe what You've said: *"My sheep hear My voice."*

Holy Spirit, tune my ears to Heaven's frequency. Highlight when You are speaking—through scripture, through thoughts, through nudges. Make me bold to respond, even when it's uncomfortable. I want to be someone You can trust with divine assignments. Teach me to hear and help me to follow. In Jesus' name, amen.

Daily Challenge (Muscle Builder #11)

Step 1: Listen on Purpose.
Set aside 10 minutes in a quiet space. Ask the Holy Spirit:

"Is there someone You want to speak to through me today?"
"Is there anything You want to say to me right now?"

Write down what you hear or sense. Don't filter or analyze it yet—just record it.

Step 2: Step Toward Obedience.
If someone comes to mind, ask God for a word of encouragement for them. Maybe it's a scripture, a phrase, or a simple "thinking of you." Then… *send it.* A text, a voice note, a prayer—even if it feels small.

Practice declaration:

"I am a sheep of the Good Shepherd. I hear His voice, and I follow Him. I am learning to listen, and I will obey."

Track it:
Write down what happened. Did you hear something? Did you reach out to someone? Did a moment of confirmation follow? These small risks are the training grounds for a Spirit-led life.

Day 12: Spoons to the Rescue

Scripture Anchor

2 Timothy 1:7 (NKJV) –

"For God has not given us a spirit of fear, but of power and of love and of a sound mind."

My Story

It was just supposed to be lunch with my parents.

We met in downtown McKinney, our usual halfway point, but the restaurant we'd planned on was closed. We wandered over to a nearby café—Spoons. The place was packed, and as we waited to be seated, I noticed something unusual.

The young hostess sitting nearby wore a Velcro brace on her knee.

My dad casually asked what happened, and she explained she was a former gymnast whose career had been cut short due to injury. She was sweet, upbeat, and clearly used to answering this question. But I wasn't satisfied with the idea that she would just live like this. The enemy had stolen something from her—and I couldn't walk away.

But fear crept in.

There were people around. It was a public place. I didn't want to make a scene, or worse, embarrass this young woman. *What if she said no? What if nothing happened?* Fear whispered all the usual lines.

As we were seated, the moment seemed to pass. But I couldn't shake it. I knew God was nudging me. And I remembered what He'd taught me before: fear doesn't protect you – obedience does. I quickly said a silent prayer to ask God for boldness and stood back up.

I walked back to the hostess stand, took a breath, and simply said:

"Hi, I'm a Christian, and sometimes when I pray for people, they get healed. Would it be okay if I prayed for your knee?"

She lit up and said, "Yes, of course!"

I placed my hand on her brace and quietly commanded the pain to go in Jesus' name. It didn't leave the first time. So I prayed again. Still some pain. She then mentioned she also had scoliosis, and I felt the stakes rise. *Now it's a back issue too?*

But I remembered: *This isn't my power—it's His.*

I placed my hands on her back and ribs and commanded alignment. She began to feel warmth. She smiled. "Maybe I'll wake up straight in the morning!" she said with a grin.

I didn't know if the healing was immediate. But I knew obedience had happened.

Later, as we were leaving the restaurant, she waved me down excitedly:

"My knee doesn't hurt anymore! I even took the brace off!"

Reflection

Fear is often the first thing that shows up when you consider stepping out in faith. It sounds like caution, humility, or "wisdom." But scripture makes it clear—**fear is not from God.**

2 Timothy 1:7 says that *power*, *love*, and a *sound mind* are the gifts of the Spirit—not fear. So when fear shows up, it's a signal: the enemy is trying to stop something powerful.

The enemy's goal is to intimidate you out of your assignment. If he can't steal your authority, he'll try to silence it. He wants you to believe you'll mess up, be embarrassed, or make someone uncomfortable.

But here's the truth: boldness doesn't mean *not* feeling fear. It means refusing to let fear make the decision.

The apostles in Acts 4 prayed not for comfort—but for boldness:

"Now, Lord... grant to Your servants that with all boldness they may speak Your word... by stretching out Your hand to heal." (Acts 4:29–30)

Boldness invites the supernatural. And obedience invites God's power into someone else's pain.

Reflective Question

What's one situation in my life today that fear has kept me from stepping out and how might obedience invite God's power into it?

Activation Prayer

Lord, thank You that You have not given me a spirit of fear. I renounce every voice that tries to intimidate me into silence. I don't need a microphone or a platform—I just need to say yes.

Holy Spirit, give me eyes to see the people You've placed in my path. Give me boldness like the early church. Help me to obey, even when my heart is racing. Even if the moment feels awkward. Even if I feel unqualified. Let me be a vessel of healing, love, and courage. In Jesus' name, amen.

Daily Challenge (Muscle Builder #12)

Step 1: Ask God to highlight one person today who needs healing, comfort, or encouragement. It could be at the grocery store, the coffee line, your office, or the gym.

Step 2: Ask God for the words to say. Start simple. Here are a few you can try:

- "Hey, this may sound random, but I felt like God wanted me to pray for you. Would that be okay?"
- "I'm a Christian and I believe God still heals today. Can I say a quick prayer for your [knee/back/head/etc.]?"

You're not responsible for the results—**you're responsible for your obedience.**

Track it: Whether you follow through or not, write down what happened. What did you sense? What got in the way? What did you learn about yourself and God?

Week 3: You Can Heal the Sick

"Jesus did not heal the sick in order to coax them to be Christians. He healed because it was His nature to heal." — ***John G. Lake***

Jesus never separated salvation from healing. Everywhere He went, He preached the Kingdom *and* healed the sick—and then He turned to His followers and said, "You can do it too." Healing isn't for a select few with microphones and ministries. It's the inheritance of every believer, because the same Spirit who raised Jesus from the dead lives in you.

This week, you'll step into the bold truth that miracles aren't rare—they're normal for those who believe. Across six powerful days, you'll:

- Step into your authority as a vessel of divine health, not just divine healing.
- Discover that your words of faith, even small ones, carry Kingdom-level power.
- Learn to pray with both reverence and guts, knowing the same Spirit who raised Christ lives in you.
- See how simple obedience and compassion can release miracles in everyday encounters.
- Grow to expect the supernatural—and take risks believing God for more than you've seen before.

By the end of these six days, you'll no longer wonder if you "qualify" to pray for the sick—you'll know that healing flows through you because Jesus lives in you.

Day 13: You Can Do It Too

Scripture Anchor

John 14:12 (NKJV) –

"Most assuredly, I say to you, he who believes in Me, the works that I do he will do also; and greater works than these he will do, because I go to My Father."

My Story

I used to believe healing ministry was reserved for a select few—pastors, missionaries, the spiritually elite. The ones with anointing oil in one hand and a Bible degree in the other.

Then I read **Mark 16:17–18 (NKJV)**:

"These signs will follow *those who believe*… they will lay hands on the sick, and they will recover."

No mention of seminary. No requirements to have your life perfectly in order. Just this:
Believe. Go. Lay hands. Expect healing.

So I did.

At first, I was nervous. Would people think I was weird? What if nothing happened? But every time I took a step—no matter how small—God met me.

I prayed for coworkers, strangers, waitresses, old friends. Sometimes healing was instant. Sometimes it came gradually. Sometimes nothing happened that I could tell. Sometimes I never saw that person again, so didn't find out what happened. But every single time, **faith grew**—in me and in them. I had to trust I was planting a seed that God would take over watering.

And now, whenever someone says, "Wow, I wish I had your gift," I smile and say:

"You do. His name is Jesus."

I remember putting this to the test by having my mom pray for my dad after he twisted his ankle stepping off a curb. I told my mom to repeat after me over the phone, while she laid hands on my dad's ankle:

"In Jesus' name, I go back in time before this injury occurred and cancel the attack by the power of the Blood of the Lamb. I call on the redemptive power of Jesus Christ, so that this injury never happened, and all symptoms and side effects of the injury are gone right now in Jesus' name. Ankle, I command you to function with God's perfect design and do your job. Ligaments, tendons, and muscles in the ankle—I command you back into the blueprint of heaven to be restored to God's perfection. Pain, go now, in Jesus' name."

"I stand on the promise of the Word that if we resist the devil, he will flee. I stand on the promise that we can tread on serpents, and nothing will by any means hurt us. I stand on the promise that if we lay hands, they will recover. Amen."

My dad did the final step by exercising his faith—getting up off the chair and walking. Jesus always did this in his healing stories—having them do something they couldn't do before—like taking up their mat to walk after being lame for a lifetime.

By the time my dad crossed to the other side of the room, with each step the pain disappeared. And the next morning, he said it was like it never occurred. Amen!

Reflection

You don't need a stage to see miracles—you just need to *believe.*

Jesus didn't say the spiritually elite would do His works. He said **"he who believes."** That's you.

And the works He referred to? Healing the sick. Casting out demons. Speaking with wisdom and power. Walking in authority. Living supernaturally.

John 14:12 isn't symbolic. It's literal.

"The works that I do, he will do also."

Let that truth shatter any insecurity or comparison in you.

If Jesus lives in you, then **His Spirit is already equipped to work through you.**

It's not about your eloquence—it's about your obedience. Not about your perfection—but your willingness.

The enemy will whisper:

- "You're not ready."

- "You don't know enough."
- "What if you mess it up?"
- "It won't work."

But God says:

"These signs will follow *those who believe.*" (Mark 16:17)

Signs follow believers—not the other way around.

Reflective Question

Where in my today is God inviting me to step out in bold faith, to lay hands on the sick, speak encouragement, or pray with authority?

Activation Prayer

Jesus, thank You that Your power isn't limited to a few—it's available to *every believer.* That means me. I don't need to wait for a special title or moment. I can start walking in faith today.

Holy Spirit, teach me to release what I've received. When You lead, I will follow. When You speak, I will obey. When You nudge, I won't delay.

I declare that the same Spirit who raised Jesus from the dead lives in me. I am qualified because You live inside me. Use my hands to heal, my words to encourage, my life to testify. In Jesus' name, amen.

Daily Challenge (Muscle Builder #13)

Step 1: Take one bold step to pray for someone today. Ask God: *"Who needs healing, comfort, or encouragement around me?"*

Then approach them with a simple question: "Would it be okay if I prayed for you?"

Step 2: Lay hands (with permission), speak short, faith-filled words.
No pressure. No theatrics. Just Jesus. Let Him do the rest.

Step 3: Rewrite your identity.
Declare this out loud:

"I am a believer. Signs follow me. Healing flows through me. I carry the power and presence of Jesus."

Track it: What did you do today that you never would've done before? That's spiritual growth.

Day 14: Miracle in the Waiting

Scripture Anchor

Mark 11:24 (NIV) –

"Therefore I tell you, whatever you ask for in prayer, believe that you have received it, and it will be yours."

My Story

For six years, Sharla and her husband tried to conceive. Each month brought fresh disappointment. If you've ever walked through infertility, you understand: there are only twelve chances a year. And every negative pregnancy test feels like another funeral for your hope. It's easy to start doubting whether God intended you to become a parent at all.

When Sharla opened up to me about her journey, I shared with her what I wish I had known sooner: that God's will is for us to be fruitful and multiply (Genesis 1:28)—and that we have authority in Jesus' name to command our bodies into alignment with heaven.

I also shared that Romans 12:2 had become one of my favorite Bible verses to remember when I am unsure of God's will, "And do not be conformed to this world, but be transformed by the renewing of your mind, that you may prove what is that good and acceptable and *perfect will of God*."

I went on to say, "If I knew then, what I know now…I would command Satan and his demons to leave my womb. I would command each child-producing organ in my body to accept God's richest blessings and operate by God's perfect design. I would resist the devil, and he would have to flee."

Sharla didn't just listen—she took it seriously. Every day, she declared healing over her womb, her eggs, and her fallopian tubes. She prayed bold prayers and commanded her body to cooperate with God's will.

Three months later, she was pregnant!

But that wasn't the only miracle. God even confirmed her pregnancy in a dream, telling her, *"Whatever you ask according to My will, I will answer. WHATEVER."*

Sometimes, we forget that God actually means what He says.

Reflection

If God's will is perfect, and He wants us to be fruitful and multiply, bringing children into this world should not be difficult. So why do so many of us struggle with infertility? Simple, we have an enemy among us.

"The thief does not come except to *steal*, and to *kill*, and to *destroy*. I have come that they may have life, and that they may have it more abundantly." (John 10:10 NKJV)

Satan and his demons have a mission – and it is to steal your destiny, kill your dreams, and destroy your future. Luckily, James 4:7 says, "*Resist the devil* and *he will flee* from you." I know now that I have the authority in Jesus' name to tell demons to leave me alone.

In all of Jesus' miracles on earth, He didn't pray to His father to heal the sick or raise the dead—he spoke God's will to the person.

"*Take up your bed and walk*" was His instruction in John 5:11 to a man healed after 38 years of infirmity.

"*Lazarus, come forth!*" was His proclamation in John 11:43 when he raised a man from the dead.

God gave us the power and authority to move mountains with our words. He told us to speak to the problem so the problem will move.

Each of us has a prayer...we each have our "whatever" we are asking God to answer. But He needs us to do our part—understand His will and command the evil to flee so God's will may freely flow.

Reflective Question

What is my "whatever" prayer today-the thing I've stopped believing for-and how might God be inviting me to speak His will and resist discouragement in the waiting?

Activation Prayer

Father, thank You for reminding me that no season is too far gone for You to move. You are the God who revives what feels dead, who brings life where there's been only disappointment. I release every timeline I've clung to, and I lay my expectations at Your feet.

Heal the places in me that have grown numb from waiting. Restore wonder to my heart. Like Sharla, I want to hope again—even when it feels risky. Teach me to believe that Your promises still stand, and that Your timing is always good.

I trust You with my story. I trust You with the wait. In Jesus' name, amen.

Daily Challenge (Muscle Builder #14)

Step 1: Write down in the space below your "whatever" that you have been consistently praying and waiting for.
What is the miracle you're asking for? Be specific.

Step 2: Declare alignment.
Speak over the area of need in your life or body and declare it must align with God's Word. Use this simple format:

"In Jesus' name, I command [body/finances/marriage] to align with God's will and function to heaven's perfect design."

Step 3: Join faith with others. Consider launching or joining a prayer challenge. Whether it's two people or twenty, stand together, share your requests, and expect praise reports.

Day 15: Healing in the Breakroom

Scripture Anchor

Matthew 10:7–8 (NIV) –

"As you go, proclaim this message: 'The kingdom of heaven has come near.' Heal the sick, raise the dead, cleanse those who have leprosy, drive out demons. Freely you have received; freely give."

My Story

We both watched as Beth's leg *shifted* to match the other.

I kept running into Beth in the breakroom—microwaves humming, vending machines buzzing. Not exactly a "spiritual" setting. But I finally asked, "Would you be okay if I prayed for you?"

She always looked tired and moved stiffly, often mentioning another doctor's appointment. For weeks, I smiled politely and wished her well—but something in my spirit kept tugging.

One day, she mentioned the doctors were recommending surgery. That's when I knew I couldn't stay silent anymore.

To my surprise, she said yes—and added quietly, "I've actually been healed through prayer before…but I lost it."

That struck me. And I felt a fire rise up. *Not this time.*

I asked her to sit down, and with her legs stretched in front of her, I could see one was visibly shorter than the other. I placed my thumbs against her ankles and prayed just as I'd seen others do in YouTube video testimonies:

"In Jesus' name, I command this left leg to grow. Spine, come into alignment. Knees and hips, do your job."

I checked her arms next—one shoulder still had pain. We prayed again.

She stood and walked smoothly across the breakroom—no limp, no pain.

"It's gone," she whispered.

That day, between vending machines and microwaves, the kingdom of Heaven showed up in a breakroom.

Reflection

Sometimes we think miracles are for Sunday mornings or spiritual superstars. But Jesus didn't say, "Heal the sick at the temple." He said, *"As you go..."*

That means healing happens in breakrooms, grocery stores, parking lots, dentist chairs—**anywhere there's a believer who knows their authority.**

Jesus gave you a command in Matthew 10:

"Heal the sick... cleanse the lepers... freely you have received, freely give."

That's not just permission—it's *commission.*

You don't need a crowd. You don't need perfect conditions. You don't even need to feel confident.

You just need to *step in.*

Beth told me she'd been healed before—but "lost it." Many people experience real healing but don't know how to stand in it. Doubt creeps in. Symptoms try to return. And they agree with the pain instead of the promise.

That's why we train our spiritual muscles. Because healing isn't just about one prayer—it's about *discipleship.* God is looking for people who won't just receive miracles, but release them.

And it doesn't have to be loud. Or dramatic. Or weird.

You just have to be **available.**

Reflective Question

Where in my life today am I tempted to agree with fear or delay, and how can I instead declare God's will and stand firm in faith?

Activation Prayer

Jesus, thank You that healing isn't something I have to earn—**it's something I get to release.** You've freely given me Your authority, and I choose to walk in it.

Forgive me for thinking I needed a certain setting or spiritual title. You told me to go and heal. And so I say: yes.

Holy Spirit, open my eyes to see the hurting around me. Give me boldness to ask, faith to speak, and humility to obey. Let breakrooms become sanctuaries. Let offices become places of outpouring. I declare that wherever I go, the Kingdom of Heaven goes with me. In Jesus' name, amen.

Daily Challenge (Muscle Builder #15)

Step 1: Identify someone in your daily environment (work, school, errands) who has shared a health need. If no one comes to mind, ask the Holy Spirit to highlight someone today.

Step 2: Ask one bold question.

"Would it be okay if I prayed for you real quick?"

Start small. You don't need a big speech—just a willing heart. Remember, this isn't about *your* power. You're just delivering the package.

Optional prayer to use:

"Pain, I command you to leave in Jesus' name. Body, come into alignment with God's perfect design. Be healed, right now."

Step 3: Reflect & Record

What happened? How did it feel to step out? Whether the healing was instant or not, write down your obedience—and God's faithfulness in the space below.

Day 16: When It Doesn't Happen Instantly

Scripture Anchor

Mark 8:25 (NIV) –

"Once more, Jesus put his hands on the man's eyes. Then his eyes were opened, his sight was restored, and he saw everything clearly."

My Story

Not every healing I've witnessed has been lightning-fast.

I've had moments where I laid hands, spoke the name of Jesus, and *boom*—pain gone. A joint popped. A tumor vanished. Someone walked without a limp. We love those stories. We celebrate them.

But there have also been the "rain" moments. Slow, steady healing that took time.

I remember one woman, Cindy, who had chronic shoulder pain that had lasted for years. We prayed together, but nothing changed. I prayed again. Still no breakthrough.

She looked at me kindly and said, "It's okay. Maybe it's just not my time."

That phrase hit me sideways. *Not your time?* I wanted to scream, *"No! It's always your time! Jesus already paid for this!"* But I held my tongue.

Later that night, I prayed again—this time alone. I reminded God of His promises and asked why nothing had shifted.

He whispered:

"Lightning or rain, the healing is already on its way."

A week later, she emailed me:

"You won't believe this. Every day, the pain has been less and less. This morning I woke up—and it's completely gone."

That healing didn't happen in the breakroom. It didn't happen with fireworks. It happened in the quiet—like rain soaking deep into the ground.

Reflection

We often assume that **fast** equals **faithful.** But healing is not about speed—it's about **completion**.

Jesus Himself didn't rush healing. In Mark 8, He prayed for a blind man and asked, *"Do you see anything?"* The man replied, *"I see people—they look like trees walking around."* So Jesus prayed again.

Even the Son of God showed us that sometimes healing is a **process**.

When healing doesn't happen instantly, the enemy loves to swoop in with lies:

- *You didn't pray right.*

- *You must not have enough faith.*
- *God's not listening.*
- *It must not be His will.*

But the Word of God says differently:

- **"They will lay hands on the sick, and they will recover."** (Mark 16:18, NKJV)
- **"By His stripes we are healed."** (Isaiah 53:5, NKJV)
- **"Ask, and it will be given to you..."** (Matthew 7:7, NKJV)

In *The Mechanics of Miracles*, Jonathan Brenneman uses a powerful analogy: healing can come like lightning or like rain.

Lightning is sudden and dramatic—a charged cloud releases its power in a flash. Through communion with God, we are like those clouds, filled with His power and ready to release it in an instant. As Paul said in Colossians 1:29 (NIV), "I strenuously contend with all the energy Christ so powerfully works in me." If Jesus lives in you, then His healing power does too—and it can be released immediately through your hands, your words, and your faith.

But sometimes, healing comes like rain. Rain is gentle. Quiet. Slow. You can't see roots growing beneath the soil, but they are. The sprouting is invisible at first—but real. Brenneman points out that many people feel no change in the moment they receive prayer, but days or weeks later, the healing is undeniable. Just like a plant after a storm, their body begins to respond.

So now, when I pray for someone and nothing seems to happen right away, I share this: *"Healing can be like lightning—or like rain."*

And I send them away with hope. Because the Word says we are healed—not by what we feel, but by what Jesus already did.

Reflective Question

Where in my life today could God be inviting me to trust His "rain process," even when results don't come instantly?

Activation Prayer

Jesus, thank You that healing is not a formula—it's a promise. I surrender the need for instant results, and instead I choose to trust Your timing.

Holy Spirit, when I don't see immediate change, help me not to retreat into disappointment or doubt. Remind me that healing can come like a lightning strike or like steady rain. Either way, it comes from You.

I declare that every prayer I've prayed in faith is heard. Every cell in my body comes into alignment with Heaven's design. I will not waver. I will not give up. I will keep watering this promise until it blossoms. In Jesus' name, amen.

Daily Challenge (Muscle Builder #16)

Step 1: Identify one healing you've been waiting on—in your body, emotions, or family. Write it down plainly in the space below.

Step 2: Speak the Word over it like rain soaking dry ground. Try:

"I thank You, Lord, that I am healed by the stripes of Jesus. Whether it's lightning or rain, healing is happening now. I receive it. I agree with it. I expect it."

Bonus: Read Mark 8:22–26 slowly.

Note how even Jesus took a second touch. Let it break off any shame about "needing more time."

Step 3: Record what changes over the next few days and record your observations.

Even a *1%* shift is worth celebrating. Healing is happening—trust the process.

Day 17: A Stranger in this Town

Scripture Anchor

Mark 16:17-18 (NKJV) –

"And these signs will follow those who believe: In My name... they will lay hands on the sick, and they will recover."

My Story

I once heard it said that if you want to see your spiritual gifts in action, go where you're a stranger—somewhere you're not held back by fear of what people think. I got to put that to the test on a business trip to another state.

At a popular restaurant one night, a young waiter brought our drinks with a big grin and a warm presence. As we chatted, he opened up about his dream of becoming an actor. Though nothing major had landed yet, he was full of hope and eager to keep trying. Eventually, he mentioned that he had been a college basketball player—and that a torn Achilles tendon had sidelined him for over a year.

He confessed that the injury was still painful and now even threatened his acting career. He was doing all he knew to do. "But I pray to God every day that He will heal me," he said with hope in his voice.

That was my cue. I didn't need further instruction.

"Well…you're doing it wrong," I said, already sliding out of my seat.

His eyes widened. "What do you mean 'doing it wrong?'"

"You're not supposed to ask God to heal you. You're supposed to *command* the healing!"

I came around to his side and looked him in the eye. "God loves you very much. He wants you well. I'd like to pray for you—and I'm going to put my hands on your ankle. It's your right one, isn't it?"

His jaw dropped. "How did you know that?"

"Because God told me," I smiled. "He wants you to know He sees you."

I placed both hands on his ankle and prayed quietly, knowing only heaven needed to hear:

"Spirit of pain, I command you to leave this ankle now in the name of Jesus Christ. Achilles tendon, in Jesus' name I command you to be healed. Spirit of God, thank You for blessing this young man with a perfect ankle."

Moments later, I started to walk back to my seat when he exclaimed, "Whoa! What did you do? My ankle feels...different. Heavy. Something's happening!"

I turned, elated. "That's God healing you! What do you feel now?"

He bounced a little. Then more. "It feels better… No! The pain is completely gone!"

He beamed, gave me a huge hug, and began bouncing down the aisle like an athlete warming up for a game.

Reflection

God loves showing off when we step out —especially when we're the least likely candidate in the room. Being a stranger doesn't disqualify you from moving in spiritual authority—it often activates it. Sometimes we hesitate because we think boldness is for pastors, preachers, or "the prayer team." But Jesus gave *all believers* the command to heal the sick. You don't need a platform—you just need a moment and obedience.

One of the ways the Holy Spirit loves to empower these moments is through a **word of knowledge**—a supernatural insight about a person or situation that we wouldn't otherwise know. It's one of the spiritual gifts Paul describes in 1 Corinthians 12:7–8 (NKJV):

"But the manifestation of the Spirit is given to each one for the profit of all: for to one is given the word of wisdom through the Spirit, to another the word of knowledge through the same Spirit..."

When God reveals something specific—like the location of pain, an emotional burden, or even a person's name—it's not to overwhelm or impress. It's to **demonstrate His nearness and care**. Words of knowledge often act as a divine appointment bell: they get the person's attention and build faith that God really sees them.

And when that moment comes, you won't need to shout or impress. Just listen, obey, and speak with the authority Jesus already gave you. A word of knowledge might be the very key that unlocks someone's healing—or their heart.

Reflective Question

When was the last time I'd sensed God giving me a "word of knowledge," and how might He be inviting me to boldly act on it next time?

Activation Prayer

Jesus, thank You for giving me power and authority in Your name. I repent for waiting to feel qualified. I say yes to Your promptings. Teach me to listen when You whisper, and to move even when I'm nervous. Let boldness rise in me—not because I'm great, but because *You* are. I want to carry miracles into restaurants, sidewalks, checkout lines, and boardrooms. Send me. I'm ready. In Jesus' name, amen.

Daily Challenge (Muscle Builder #17)

Step 1: Be open to unfamiliar settings.

Ask the Holy Spirit to give you one moment today where you're the "stranger with authority.

Step 2: Pay attention to words of knowledge—body pain, highlighted areas, or sudden empathy. Ask God, "What are You showing me?"

Step 3: Offer prayer boldly.
Command healing. Don't overthink it. Just say what He says—and then let heaven do what only it can do.

Declaration:

"I am not a spectator—I'm a carrier of power.
Even as a stranger, I carry the name of Jesus.
Healing follows me, even when I least expect it."

Day 18: God of Generations

Scripture Anchor

John 10:10 (NKJV) –

"The thief does not come except to steal, and to kill, and to destroy. I have come that they may have life, and that they may have it more abundantly."

My Story

Charlotte called to tell me the cyst was completely gone. The doctor declared her daughter healed. No surgery. No loss. No delay to her future.

Weeks before I ran into Charlotte at a Tex-Mex restaurant in the middle of Oklahoma—after not seeing her for over 20 years. I'd randomly chosen this stop on a long drive home from a healing conference. I certainly didn't expect to be greeted by her at the hostess stand. But God knew.

After some joyful catching up, she came by our table and shared something heavier. Her 18-year-old daughter had a 5mm cyst on her ovary, and doctors were considering removing it. Fear hung over her future.

I asked if I could pray.

Right there in the restaurant, Charlotte placed her hands on her own ovaries to represent her daughter. I laid hands on hers and prayed: first commanding the spirit of infirmity to go, then declaring healing over her daughter's ovaries. But then something unexpected poured out—words reclaiming her daughter's *future* children. A prophetic declaration that the enemy could not steal her destiny or legacy.

Reflection

God cares about more than symptoms—He cares about legacy. In Scripture, healing is often tied to *restoration*—not only of the body, but of destiny. What began as a simple healing prayer for a cyst became a declaration that a daughter's future children would not be stolen.

When you speak with Holy Spirit-led authority, your words can do more than bring relief—they can **prophesy alignment with Heaven's design**. Proverbs 18:21 reminds us that *"death and life are in the power of the tongue"*—and when we speak life over someone's future, we are not guessing…we are partnering with God's intention.

In that Tex-Mex restaurant, God wasn't just healing a body. He was reinstating a generational promise.

That's the power of prophetic declaration. You don't need to be a prophet to speak prophetically. When you sense what God wants to do—and you boldly agree with it out loud—you're giving permission for Heaven to invade Earth.

What is an area where the enemy has tried to steal from you? Health, joy, legacy, children, time? Use John 10:10 as your anchor and speak God's abundant life over it in Jesus' name. He's not just restoring your now…He's redeeming your next.

Reflective Question

What area of my life or family today has the enemy tried to steal and how could God be inviting me to boldly declare His abundant life over it?

Activation Prayer

Lord, thank You that You go before me and prepare divine appointments. I yield to Your nudges, even when they seem random. I ask for boldness to speak what You speak. I declare that no assignment of the enemy can steal what You have planned. Use me to call forth life, healing, and future over every person I meet.

Interrupt my day. Disrupt my routine. I give You permission to use my "ordinary" for something eternal. In Jesus' name, amen.

Daily Challenge (Muscle Builder #18)

Step 1: Ask God for a divine appointment today—even in unexpected places. Say, "God, interrupt me with purpose." Before entering any public space today, pray:

"Holy Spirit, highlight someone I can encourage, bless, or pray for today."

Step 2: Pray over someone's future.
Don't just pray for healing—ask God what their destiny holds and pray that nothing would stand in its way.

Step 3: Journal the moment in the space below.
What did you see? What did you feel? What did you say or pray? The more you track it, the more aware you'll become of how often God is moving around you.

Declaration:

"Where the enemy tried to steal, God is restoring. I carry the authority to protect legacies and release healing. God has prepared a table—and I will show up ready. Every space I enter is an opportunity for God to move through me."

Week 4: Listen & Obey

"God doesn't call the qualified—He qualifies the called. Obedience is simply saying yes and letting Him do the rest." — *Anonymous (paraphrased by A.W. Tozer)*

The Christian life isn't just about hearing God's voice—it's about responding. Miracles happen on the other side of simple obedience. Every nudge, every whisper, every inconvenient assignment is an opportunity for Heaven to invade Earth. You don't have to be fearless or perfect—you just have to be willing.

Over this coming week, you'll:

- Learn to pause for the one-person God highlights, even in unexpected places.
- Recognize divine interruptions as opportunities, not inconveniences.
- Discover how faith and compassion can release power into someone else's need.
- Grow in confidence that obedience matters more than eloquence.
- Experience the joy of being part of someone else's answered prayer.
- Realize that your "yes" can ripple far beyond the moment you give it.

By the end of these six days, you'll see that obedience is not about obligation—it's about partnership. When you listen and obey, you step into the adventure of living as Jesus lived: interruptible, available, and full of power.

Day 19: The Woman in the Lobby

Scripture Anchor

Acts 3:6 (NIV) –

"Then Peter said, 'Silver or gold I do not have, but what I do have I give you. In the name of Jesus Christ of Nazareth, walk.'"

My Story

I was leaving an event—tired, hungry, and ready to head home.

As I stepped into the lobby, I spotted a woman standing alone, slightly hunched, with a brace on her wrist. I smiled and walked past.

But the Holy Spirit whispered:

"Turn around. She's the one."

I paused. *Not now, Lord... I'm tired. Maybe someone else?*

Again, the nudge. So I turned back.

"Hi," I said gently. "I couldn't help but notice your brace. Are you in pain? Would it be okay if I prayed for you?"

Tears immediately welled up in her eyes. She nodded.

I laid my hand over hers and invited the presence of Jesus. I didn't yell. I didn't quote a dozen scriptures. I just prayed from compassion and confidence in His name.

After a moment, she moved her hand slowly. Then again.

"It doesn't hurt anymore," she whispered. "What just happened?"

"Jesus sees you," I said. "And He heals."

She had walked into that lobby expecting nothing. But Heaven had other plans—and all it took was **someone willing to stop.**

Reflection

Sometimes the most supernatural moments happen **on your way out.** Have you ever felt that nudge—that tug on your spirit—when someone catches your eye, but you keep walking anyway? I have. And more often than not, I'm left with the quiet sting of regret, wondering what God might have done if I had just stopped. That's why I try to remember that feeling—not to shame myself, but to let it train me. I want to be the kind of person who responds in the moment, who lets the Holy Spirit interrupt my plans. Because on the other side of that small yes could be someone's answered prayer.

The woman in the lobby didn't have a sign on her that said, *"Pray for me."* But the Holy Spirit knew. And He was looking for someone interruptible.

Acts 3 gives us a beautiful example. Peter and John were headed into the temple. Routine. Normal. But at the gate called Beautiful, they saw a lame man. And Peter said:

"What I have, I give you. In Jesus' name—walk."

He didn't offer a formula. He didn't wait for backup. He offered **what he carried.**

You may not feel prepared. You might feel like you have nothing to offer.

But if you carry Jesus—you carry **enough.**

The key isn't your energy level or your eloquence—it's your *availability.* The Holy Spirit doesn't just move when you feel strong. He moves when you say yes.

Reflective Question

Where in my life today could God be nudging me to pause and say yes-especially moments when I feel tired or distracted and how could that small act of availability become someone's miracle?

Activation Prayer

Jesus, thank You that ministry doesn't only happen on stages or during scheduled moments. It happens in lobbies. In hallways. In checkout lines. At the exact moment someone needs to know they're seen.

Holy Spirit, I want to be interruptible. Open my eyes to the people around me—even when I feel tired, distracted, or unsure. Use my hands, my words, and my willingness.

I say yes to the nudge. I say yes to the assignment. I say yes to the one.
In Jesus' name, amen.

Daily Challenge (Muscle Builder #19)

Step 1: Pay attention to your "passing" moments today.
As you leave a room, finish a meeting, or walk to your car—ask:

"Holy Spirit, is there someone I'm meant to stop for?"

Step 2: Act on the nudge.
It may be prayer, a conversation, or even a smile that says, *"You're seen."* Don't underestimate the impact.

Step 3: Reflect.
What did you sense? What did the person say or feel? Write it down in the space below.

Declaration:

"I don't miss the moment. I carry Heaven—even on the way out."

Day 20: Go Find the One

Scripture Anchor

Luke 15:4 (NIV) –

"Suppose one of you has a hundred sheep and loses one of them. Doesn't he leave the ninety-nine in the open country and go after the lost sheep until he finds it?"

My Story

One day, I heard God whisper something unexpected:

"I want you to go to Target."

At first, I laughed. *Really, Lord? You're sending me shopping?*

But the tug was undeniable. So, I got in the car and prayed:

"Okay, if You're sending me, who am I going for?"

As I walked through the store, I kept listening.

Nothing at first.

Then I passed a woman standing alone in the home goods section. She looked…*heavy.* Not in body, but in spirit. Her face carried something—grief, anxiety, maybe just exhaustion.

The whisper came again:

"She's the one."

So I walked over gently and said:

“Hi, I know this might sound strange, but I feel like God sent me here for you. Are you okay?”

Tears. Right there by the throw pillows.

She had just received bad news about her child’s health. She didn’t believe in coincidences, and she definitely didn’t believe it was random that I showed up.

I got to pray with her. Bless her. Speak peace and healing over her situation.

Then I left—with nothing in my cart…but a heart full of awe.

Reflection

Jesus is always looking for **the one.**

The lost one. The hurting one. The skeptical one. The overlooked one. The one who’s secretly asking, *“God, do You even see me?”*

He saw them then. He sees them now. And often? **He wants to send you.**

Luke 15:4 reminds us that the Good Shepherd leaves the 99 to find the one—not because the 99 don’t matter, but because the one is *hurting alone.*

The Spirit-led life isn’t just about sensing God’s presence—it’s about responding to His **direction.**

Sometimes, He'll say, "Speak to that person", or "Pay for their groceries." Sometimes just smile and ask how they are.

You never know what *one small act* might unlock for someone else.

And yes, it might feel inconvenient. And no, I'm not perfect and don't always obey. It will stretch your comfort zone. But remember this: **someone's breakthrough may be waiting on your obedience.**

Reflective Question

Who in my life today could be the "one" God is highlighting around me, and how can I step out in obedience, even if it feels inconvenient or unexpected?

Activation Prayer

Jesus, thank You that You came after me when I was the one. When I was hurting, confused, or drifting—you pursued me.

Now I ask You to give me that same heart. Show me who's around me, hiding in plain sight. Give me eyes to see the one You want to love through me today.

Holy Spirit, train my ears to hear Your nudges and my feet to follow them—whether it's a text, a conversation, or a spontaneous trip to Target. I want to live sent.
Use me to go after the one. In Jesus' name, amen.

Daily Challenge (Muscle Builder #20)

Step 1: Ask God to highlight one person today who feels forgotten, discouraged, or alone. Write their name below.

Step 2: Take one bold action to reach them.

- Send a voice note.
- Ask how they're *really* doing.
- Offer to pray.
- Walk across the room—or the parking lot.

Step 3: Journal what happened.
Even if it felt small or awkward—write it down in the space below. You planted a seed. You followed the Shepherd.

Declaration:

"I live sent. I go after the one. I'm ready, willing, and available."

Day 21: Who Touched Me?

Scripture Anchor

Luke 8:46 (NIV) –

"But Jesus said, 'Someone touched me; I know that power has gone out from me.'"

My Story

I wasn't even in the same room.

Michael was at home, recovering from cancer treatments. I was sitting with his good friend, Shelly, when we began to talk about how he was doing—and how much pain he was in.

I asked Shelly if I could lay hands on her as a stand-in for her friend, Michael. As we began to pray together, something unusual happened.
I felt the pain.
Not emotionally—*physically.*
A sharp pain struck the left side of my body behind my ribs, mimicking the exact symptoms she'd just described in Michael. I hadn't been feeling it before. It wasn't mine. But in that moment, I knew what was happening:

God was letting me feel what needed to be healed.

So, I kept praying. Speaking the Word. Declaring healing. And with each phrase—each declaration—the pain in my own body began to lift.

After we finished, Shelly called Michael. She didn't say much—just asked how he was feeling.
He paused.
Then said, "Actually…I'm feeling great. The pain is gone."

Later that week, tests confirmed a dramatic improvement. Healing had begun.

It was one of the clearest moments I've ever experienced of the Holy Spirit's power flowing—through me, yes, but also *to* me. It reminded me of the story in Luke 8—the woman who pushed through the crowd just to *touch the hem* of Jesus' robe. And when she did, He didn't say, *"Who bumped into me?"*
He said, **"Who touched me?"**

Like Jesus in Luke 8, I knew that power had gone out.

Because someone had touched Him.
And this time, that someone was *me*—on Michael's behalf.

There's a difference between brushing by Jesus…and **reaching for Him in faith.**

Reflection

The woman in Luke 8 had been bleeding for 12 years. She had tried everything. Spent everything. And yet… she *believed.*

So she reached out—not with entitlement, but **with desperation.** And Jesus felt it.

"Power has gone out from me."

Here's the wild part: she didn't ask permission.
She didn't wait for her name to be called.
She didn't stop to wonder, *"Am I worthy?"*

She just touched. And power responded. Jesus stopped mid-stride and asked, "Who touched Me?" The disciples were confused—everyone was pressing in. But Jesus wasn't talking about a crowd bump. He was talking about *faith.*

Faith that draws power.
Faith that pulls Heaven to earth.
Faith that doesn't wait for perfect timing or conditions.

Too many of us stand in the crowd, watching others receive breakthrough, thinking:

- *Maybe one day it'll be my turn.*
- *I don't want to be too bold.*
- *What if nothing happens?*

But faith doesn't wait to be noticed. Faith **reaches.**

That day with Shelly, I experienced something I didn't expect: intercession that became *incarnation.* I felt the need so strongly in my body, I couldn't help but respond in prayer—and when the pain left me, it left Michael too.

The same Spirit who raised Jesus from the dead lives in you (Romans 8:11). He may stir you through compassion, a whisper, or even a physical sensation—so don't dismiss what you feel. Instead, **ask Him what He's doing—and join in.**

Reflective Question

Where in my life today could God be inviting me to move from simply being in the crowd to reaching out in faith-believing His power will respond?

Activation Prayer

Jesus, thank You that You respond to faith. Not formulas. Not volume. Just faith.
I don't want to brush by You—I want to reach with intention. I want to touch the hem of Your garment today.

I open myself fully to You—mind, body, and spirit. If You choose to speak through what I feel, I won't ignore it or explain it away. Holy Spirit, teach me to discern what's mine and what's Yours, and give me boldness to pray until pain lifts, symptoms bow, and lives are changed. I say yes to being a vessel of healing—even from a distance. In Jesus' name, amen.

Daily Challenge (Muscle Builder #21)

Step 1: Pay attention to pain. Ask the Holy Spirit to heighten your awareness of others' pain—physical, emotional, or spiritual.

Step 2: Seek the person it belongs to. If you sense discomfort or heaviness that isn't yours, pause and ask: *Is this for prayer?*

Step 3:

Read Luke 8:40–48.

Picture yourself in the woman's place. What would your "touch" look like today? Write your answer in the space below.

Declaration:

"I carry healing power in Jesus' name. Whether near or far, my prayers are effective and Spirit-led. I don't wait for permission—I reach for the hem in faith."

Day 22: Divine Delays

Scripture Anchor

Romans 8:28 (NIV) –

"And we know that in all things God works for the good of those who love him, who have been called according to his purpose."

My Story

During a recent vacation, our final leg of our flight was cancelled due to weather. The rebooking options were bleak, it was a holiday weekend, and we found ourselves seven hours from our destination with no choice but to rent a car.

After paying a frustratingly high price for a rental car, we developed an elaborate plan to return that rental and get to the original car company we intended to rent from. Our journey involved an hour-long Uber ride between airports. I was tired, frustrated, and not in the mood for divine appointments.

But our driver, Kazi, started talking almost immediately. He shared that he only had one kidney, was on dialysis, and in pain 24/7. My empathy meter was low…until I felt a sharp pain in my *own* left kidney; it felt like someone reached through my body and squeezed. I knew from experience this is one-way God points out healing needs to me—I feel the person's pain. In this case, it was not going away.

I relented and told Kazi I'd like to pray for him once we arrived. He was open—most people in pain are willing to try anything.

At the airport, I had him place his hands where both kidneys should be. I laid my hands over his and began to pray. I commanded the pain to leave and even dared to ask for a new kidney to supernaturally manifest where it had been removed. Why not? Jesus said to ask for ANYTHING in His name!

After the first prayer, Kazi said the pain lessened. After the second, it dropped further. And after the third, it was gone completely. He hadn't been pain-free in years. Though a Hindu, he gave praise to a God he didn't necessarily know, because he had encountered His love.

In that moment it hit me: What feels inconvenient to you might be the moment someone else has been praying for. Your delay may be divine—and your obedience, the bridge to someone's breakthrough. What seemed like a disruption became a divine assignment. What felt like a delay was actually a setup—for Kazi's healing and for my obedience.

Reflection

Sometimes the things that frustrate us most—canceled plans, closed doors, delays—are the very moments God is working *for* us and *through* us. He may be rerouting you—quite literally—for someone else's miracle.

Romans 8:28 reminds us that in *all things*, God is working for our good. Not just in church services or mountaintop moments—but in long car rides, missed flights, and Uber rides with strangers.

God doesn't waste anything. He reroutes with purpose.

What feels inconvenient to you might be an answer to someone else's desperate prayer. Your delay may be divine.

Reflective Question
What current "delay" in my life today might actually be a divine setup for God to work through me?

Activation Prayer

Father, thank You for being present in every detour. When things go off script, help me remember that Your plans are greater than mine. Forgive me for resisting interruptions when they could be Your invitation. Teach me to see delays not as obstacles, but as opportunities. Use me to bring healing—even in places that feel dry or disjointed. I surrender to Your reroutes, because I trust You always know where the one is. In Jesus' name, amen.

Daily Challenge (Muscle Builder #22)

Step 1: Ask the Holy Spirit to make you interruptible today. Surrender your schedule, preferences, and convenience. Invite Him to open your eyes to hidden assignments.

Step 2: Pay close attention to unexpected detours. Instead of frustration, ask: "Lord, is there someone here for me to see?".

Step 3: If prompted, offer prayer or encouragement to someone around you.
It doesn't have to be fancy—just available. You may be the only Jesus they encounter today.

Declaration:

"Even when I'm delayed, I am not derailed. I carry Heaven on the road—and miracles follow me wherever I go."

Day 23: Carriers of His Presence

Scripture Anchor

1 Corinthians 6:19 (NKJV) –

"Or do you not know that your body is the temple of the Holy Spirit who is in you, whom you have from God, and you are not your own?"

My Story

A few years ago, I watched a healing video on YouTube by Pete Cabrera Jr. that changed my life.

Pete wasn't shouting. He wasn't laying hands. He wasn't even praying out loud. He simply walked through a Walmart parking lot, releasing God's presence with every step.

As he talked to people, healing happened—**in silence.** No prayers, no laying hands. It was as if his very shadow carried glory.

I remembered the story from Acts 5:

"So that they brought the sick out into the streets…that at least the shadow of Peter passing by might fall on some of them…and they were all healed."

(Acts 5:15–16 NKJV)

Could that really happen today?

Jesus promised, "Most assuredly, I say to you, he who believes in Me, the works that I do he will do also; and greater works than these he will do, because I go to My Father." (John 14:12 NKJV). Peter believed Him and so did modern-day Pete. If they could take Jesus at His word and walk in power…so can I.

Not long after, I found myself in a dentist's chair. The hygienist, Angela, shared that she was exhausted. Something about her voice tugged at my spirit.

She casually mentioned upcoming medical tests and a biopsy on her thyroid. As she cleaned my teeth, I didn't say much, but I began praying quietly in my spirit: *"Holy Spirit, rest on her. Dissolve those nodules. Make Your healing presence known."*

Angela started crying while she was cleaning my teeth without knowing why. I let her know I was already praying for her healing and immediately said she felt different. Her neck was flushed with divine power that penetrated her neck. Her neck flooded with warmth – as if something unseen was moving through her body. It was obvious God was at work.

After I left, I prayed again: *"Lord, I laid hands with my words and my faith. Now You do what only You can do."*

A week later, Angela's tests came back: **no cancer.** The nodules had disappeared.

God reminded me: *You don't just bring Me with you. I go in you, and I move through you.*

Reflection

You are not ordinary.

When you gave your life to Jesus, the Spirit of the Living God took up residence in you. That means you are now a **mobile sanctuary**—a walking, breathing, praying vessel of His presence.

God is looking for us to be His instruments, to bring healing to those we encounter in our daily lives. You don't have to wait until church on Sunday to feel close to God. The veil was torn. The curtain is gone. The presence that once rested on the Ark of the Covenant now resides in **you.**

Colossians 1:27 says: *"Christ in you, the hope of glory."*

Not Christ next to you. Not Christ at your church. **Christ in you.**

This means the atmosphere changes when you enter a room—not because of your personality, but because of the Person you carry.

You can walk into a hospital, a workplace, a grocery store, a classroom—and healing can begin just because you're there.

This isn't mystical—it's biblical.

God's presence rests on people who host Him well. That doesn't require perfection; it requires surrender. Sensitivity. A heart that says: *"I'm available."*

When you walk with that awareness, miracles no longer feel impossible. They start feeling natural.

Reflective Question

Where is one ordinary place in my life today where God may be inviting me to carry His presence with new awareness this week?

Activation Prayer

Holy Spirit, I thank You that I am not alone—not ever. You dwell in me. You move through me. You rest upon me. I am Your temple.

Forgive me for forgetting that You are always present. Forgive me for shrinking back or waiting for someone "more spiritual" to show up. You are not confined to buildings, pulpits, or professionals. You chose *me.*

I yield my body, my voice, and my space to You. Let Your presence radiate from me—so that when people encounter me, they encounter You. Let peace displace chaos, healing displace pain, and light displace darkness—*because I carry You.* In Jesus' name, amen.

Daily Challenge (Muscle Builder #23)

Step 1: Shift your perspective.

Before walking into any space today—your office, a store, your home—pause and declare:

"The Holy Spirit lives in me. I shift the atmosphere everywhere I go."

Step 2: Practice silent intercession.

Pick one space to intentionally host God's presence. Ask Him to fill the room. Silently pray for those around you. Expect Him to move—even without words.

Step 3: Journal what happens in the space below.

Did someone comment on the peace around you? Did a moment of tension dissolve? Did God prompt you to take further action?

You are never empty. You carry the King.

Day 24: God Was Already There

Scripture Anchor

Matthew 18:18–19 (NIV) –

"Truly I tell you, whatever you bind on earth will be bound in heaven, and whatever you loose on earth will be loosed in heaven...if two of you on earth agree about anything they ask for, it will be done for them by my Father in heaven."

My Story

A good friend of mine reached out and introduced me to Nancy, a childhood friend who had just been diagnosed with a brain tumor. As she gathered people to pray, she thought of me and asked if I'd be willing to connect. Of course, I said yes.

Nancy and I lived on opposite sides of the country, so we prayed over the phone. I didn't know where the tumor was located, but as we prayed, I told her I sensed it in her forehead—right in the front of her brain. She later confirmed that was exactly where it was. I prayed boldly for the tumor to dissolve. In my imagination, I could see it breaking apart and disappearing, even though the physical evidence hadn't caught up yet.

She still moved forward with surgery, but when the doctor opened her up and got to the tumor site, he discovered something baffling: the tumor had melted. It had literally liquefied and begun to drain on its own. No cutting into delicate brain tissue. No complications.

When Nancy read the surgical report later, it matched the vision I had seen weeks before.
Not only was the tumor gone, but the pathology report showed *no cancer*. Nancy was healed—completely. And as a bonus, her doctor declared she should expect to live at least into her 80s. She had just turned 50.

Sometimes God heals without doctors. Sometimes He heals *through* them. But no matter how He chooses, when we agree in faith, something always moves.

Reflection

When you say yes to intercession, you're not just sending up a request. You're **partnering with Heaven to shift reality.**

Matthew 18 tells us that agreement is powerful. When two believers unite in faith, **something unlocks.**

Sometimes the greatest miracles aren't about whether something disappears—but *how* it disappears. Nancy still walked into the operating room. But she walked in with a different reality already at work—one that the scans hadn't yet caught up to. The world said "brain surgery." Heaven said "already handled."

This kind of healing confounds logic and glorifies God. And it reminds us that faith isn't always about seeing *nothing* go wrong—it's about seeing God's hand in the middle of what could have gone terribly wrong. When we pray, we partner with the One who sees the full timeline. And even when surgery isn't cancelled, the outcome can be transformed.

Don't underestimate the power of your voice.

Reflective Question

Who in my life today might be waiting for someone to agree with them in prayer- and could God be inviting me to be that voice of agreement this week?

Activation Prayer

Jesus, thank You that You gave me authority—not to control outcomes, but to agree with Your will. Thank You for letting me stand in the gap for others.

Holy Spirit, teach me to pray boldly. Not just emotionally—but strategically. Show me what Heaven is saying, so I can say it too.

I declare that my prayers shift atmospheres. I'm not helpless. I'm not hoping—I'm partnering. Use my voice to cancel diagnoses, release healing, and establish peace.

In Jesus' name, amen.

Daily Challenge (Muscle Builder #24)

Step 1: Ask God, "Who do You want me to intercede for today?"
Write down the name(s) in the space below that come to mind.

Step 2: Ask, "What's Heaven saying about this?"
Wait. Listen. If you sense a word, a verse, or a declaration—
write it down and pray it aloud.

Step 3: If led, share it with the person.
Encourage them. Let them know someone is standing with them in faith.

Declaration:

"My prayers aren't empty—they're echoing Heaven. I pray with bold agreement and watch things shift."

You Did It!

Scripture Anchor

Philippians 1:6 (NIV) –

"Being confident of this, that He who began a good work in you will carry it on to completion until the day of Christ Jesus."

Reflection

You've reached the end of this journey-but really, this is only the beginning.

Thirty days of stretching your faith. Opening your heart. Choosing to believe for more. You didn't just read words on a page—you activated your spirit, rewired your thinking, and invited Heaven to invade your everyday.

You learned to:

- Hear God's voice with clarity
- Minister healing with boldness
- Walk in identity, not insecurity
- Carry peace into chaos
- Speak truth over your body and circumstances
- And… receive. Fully. Freely. Joyfully.

You didn't arrive here because you were perfect. You got here because you kept showing up. Kept reaching. Kept saying, *"Yes, Lord."*

And the best part?
This is only the beginning.

God didn't lead you through this journey just to give you good stories. He did it to mark you. To transform you. To send you.

You're not just someone who *believes in the supernatural.* You're someone who *lives it.*

You are His daughter. His son. His vessel.
And as you walk forward from here, know this:

You carry the Kingdom.

So whether you're in the grocery store or the hospital room, in the quiet place or the chaos—you're never alone, and you're never powerless.

The world doesn't just need people who believe in the supernatural. The world needs people who live it. That's you.

Now go.
Live simple.
Live full.
Live *supernaturally.*

Final Commissioning Prayer

Father, thank You for walking with me through this journey. Thank You for stretching my faith, renewing my mind, and awakening my heart.

I declare that I am not the same person I was on Day 1. I've encountered You in fresh ways. I've seen Your hand. I've heard Your voice. And I've responded in obedience.

Holy Spirit, seal this work in me. Let it bear lasting fruit. When I forget, remind me. When I hesitate, nudge me. When I shrink back, pull me forward in love.

Jesus, I choose to live like You—full of compassion, full of courage, full of power.

I say yes to the supernatural life—not because I've earned it, but because You gave it.

I'm ready.
Let Heaven come through me.
In Your mighty name, amen.

Keep Going: Resources That Fueled My Journey

If this 4-week devotional lit a fire in your spirit, don't stop here. Below are some of the most powerful tools, books, and teachers that helped me embrace a supernatural lifestyle and walk in divine authority:

Books

- **"Healing in the Spirit Made Simple"** by *Praying Medic* Straightforward and inspiring—this book unpacks how to see, hear, and move in the spirit.
- **"The Power That Changes the World"** by *Bill Johnson* A powerful call to partner with God's Kingdom mindset and transform culture through supernatural love and authority.
- **"Living in God's Power"** by *John G. Lake* Collected teachings and testimonies from one of history's boldest healing evangelists, filled with faith, fire, and spiritual hunger.

Training

- **Divine Healing Technician Training®** by *Curry Blake of John G. Lake Ministries,* www.JGLM.org This course revolutionized my understanding of divine healing and authority. I recommend watching all the trainings available through this ministry—it's worth every minute to learn your true identity in Christ.
- **Pete Cabrera Jr.**, founder of *Royal Family International*, www.royalfamilyinternational.com

Pete's hands-on healing training taught me how to minister healing with boldness and simplicity. His healing testimonies on YouTube inspired me deeply, as he approached strangers in a Walmart parking lot and healed them without prayer—just presence and authority.

Kingdom Declarations

Speak these aloud daily to align with the Holy Spirit and activate your authority in Jesus Christ:

- I carry the Kingdom. Everywhere I go, Heaven goes too.
- The same Spirit who raised Jesus from the dead lives in me.
- Healing is mine—and I release it in Jesus' name.
- I don't wait for breakthrough. I release it.
- I hear God's voice clearly. I recognize His nudges and respond in faith.
- I don't need to be loud to be powerful. I need to be aligned.
- Fear is not my master. I am rooted in God's peace, grounded in truth, and led by the Holy Spirit.
- I speak life. My words carry healing, clarity, and authority.
- My hands are healing hands. My prayers move mountains.
- I am not powerless. I am not passive. I am filled with fire and led by love.
- Miracles are normal for me, because Jesus lives in me.
- I don't chase signs—they follow me.
- I am not disqualified. I am chosen, anointed, and assigned.
- I was made for this. And I say yes.

THE EVIDENCE: What God Did During These 4 Weeks

You didn't just read—you responded. This space is for the testimonies, answered prayers, and holy surprises that unfolded as you stepped out in faith.

Don't let them fade. Write them down. Remember them. They're evidence of Heaven on Earth.

About the Author

Holly Bogdan is the voice behind *My Simple, Yet Supernatural Life* (supernaturallifeblog.wordpress.com), where she shares stories of God's presence breaking into everyday life. A lifelong believer, her faith was reawakened by a personal encounter with the Holy Spirit that sparked a passion to minister healing in restaurants, offices, and grocery store aisles—proving that miracles aren't confined to church walls.

In addition to *The Authority Effect*, Holly is the author of *Modern Sarah*, a contemporary retelling of the biblical story of Sarah and Abrham, that encourages women to trust God's promises in the waiting.

She lives in the Dallas–Fort Worth area, where she balances a corporate career, family life, and ministry. Holly's mission is simple: to equip believers to recognize the authority they already carry in Christ and to step confidently into the supernatural life Jesus promised.

www.ingramcontent.com/pod-product-compliance
Lightning Source LLC
LaVergne TN
LVHW010918110826
845149LV00013B/2419
* 9 7 9 8 9 9 9 7 0 9 1 1 0 *